# Earth Render
The art of clay plaster, render and paints

# James Henderson
With illustrations by Mike Angliss
Foreword by Peter Hickson
President, Earth Building Association of Australia

# Acknowledgments

This is the book I wanted 20 years ago. It has only been possible through the help and kindness of many people.

To thank a few ...
All the clients I have had in my life that have trusted in me and the gifts of straw & clay.
Peter Cowman for layout, passion, editing and intellectual support.
Mike Angliss for all the hard work over the years and an incredible artistic talent.
Bill Steen for showing me the depth and passion of the craft.
Carol Crews for being a shining light who shares the passion of the craft.
Frank Thomas for his skill and incredible knowledge. You have taught me so much.
Peter Hickson for placing this work in its historical context.
Alanna Moore at Python Press for believing in this book.
And all of you that share the joys of straw and clay!

James Henderson
August 2013

**PYTHON PRESS**

© James Henderson 2013
© Illustrations, Mike Angliss

This edition published 2016

The moral right of the author has been asserted.

In the preparation of this information every endeavour has been made to ensure that the information supplied is correct. The author and the publisher cannot, in any way, be under any legal liability of any kind in respect of or arising out of the contents or any error therein or for the reliance any person may place upon it. .

Note: Clay may contain respirable crystalline silica and may cause respiratory, skin and eye irritation. Wear a dust mask suitable for particulates when exposed to clay dust.

All rights reserved. No part of this book may be reproduced in any form or by any electronic or mechanical means, including information storage and retrieval systems, without written permission from the publisher or author, except in the case of a reviewer, who may quote brief passages embodied in critical articles or in a review.

Printed on acid free paper by Lightning Source
Lightning Source Inc., an Ingram Content Group Inc. company, is committed to manufacturing books in a manner that both respects the environment and helps preserve the world's natural resources.

ISBN 978-0-9757782-0-3

Published by:
Python Press

EMail:
pythonpress@gmail.com

Web:
pythonpress.com

# Foreword

Building with raw unfired earth, or what we call earth building, has existed for almost long as man has built himself shelter. Archaeologists, working excavations in Jericho, have documented towns and cities built of earth dating back 9,000 to 11,000 years.

Today two to three billion people continue to occupy earth buildings or build and maintain earth buildings traditions. Of course many earth builders are self-builders rather than building professionals. Vernacular designs, traditions and earth building techniques have been evolved and developed through trial and error and happenstance by diverse, separate groups of people living in various climates, with different needs, resources, cultures and facing various local challenges or hazards. Some of us have long believed there is so much to learn and gain by exploring this rich diversity and inheritance of earth building. We believe we can build on this accumulated ancient wisdom, this legacy of mankind, to tread a more sustainable path into the future.

The key is to explore earth building traditions and vernacular building designs that match your needs, climate, resources or skills because as the old book says "there is nothing new under the sun". Today, for billions of self-builders, sustainable building means traditional shelter. For those living in unsustainably developed countries wanting to make a valuable, conscious choice - to live within the earth's means - there is a movement called Natural Building. Natural Building explores more appropriate, sustainable and renewable building technologies and principles including choosing locally sourced natural materials such as earth, stone, timber, straw and bamboo. These materials are abundant or renewable and require little processing and have extremely low embodied energy figures.

A recent unexpected and to many unexplained and unreasonable focus on sealing and insulating buildings for improved efficiency has lead professional earth builders and self-builders in Australia's colder climates to reassess and explore how they build to meet new standards. Good climate responsive design principles used in conjunction with traditional uninsulated mudbrick and rammed earth walls haven't been enough to satisfy building codes, standards and the predictions of mandatory energy assessment tools. This being the case even though existing earth buildings have been proven to be energy efficient and the low embodied energy credentials of earth buildings are exemplary.

Some earth builders including James Henderson have explored the use of the lightest and better insulating earth building techniques such as light earth (clay/straw), popular in northern Europe. Others have moved to strawbale walls, insulated stud frames or added insulation to the earth walls. I believe another solution for colder climates could be lighter weight mudbricks and low-density cob. Both clay/straw, strawbale and to a lesser extent cob have necessitated application of something new to the modern Australian earth building traditions - thick renders over uneven walls. The best practical, healthy and appropriate choice being clay/straw daubing mixtures for filling holes and building wall thickness and clay/sand earth renders for finishing surfaces.

The same approach of sealing and insulating buildings for energy efficiency in the much colder northern hemisphere climates in the UK, USA and Europe produced problems such as interstitial condensation and decay of buildings, growth of harmful mould and sick building syndrome. Paradoxically, the approach also highlighted and brought a renewed focus on healthy indoor air quality. From research we have since learned about the many other healthy beneficial attributes of earth walls. The health concerns brought about by sealing buildings has lead to a demand for earth rendering on concrete, fired brick and plasterboard plus the wider use of non-toxic clay and lime paints.

James Henderson has learned the same lessons, experienced the same joy, made the same discoveries and observations and eventually reached the same point of successful application that earth builders have done all over the world over the past 11,000 years. Of course he hasn't had to learn from scratch, in isolation because he has built on the wisdom and experience of many others from around the world who in turn had explored the practices of traditional builders. He has read, listened and learned from a wide variety of sources and then applied this knowledge as a builder and tradesman applying and honing his craft over time. Now he is now keen and very capable of sharing his passion and experience with others on the same journey.

As James himself acknowledges, this is the book he wanted 20 years ago. This is not a coffee table book, nor an academic text. It is an extremely well written and easily understood practical manual. It would be a valuable addition to your library whether you are a self-builder, student of earth building techniques or an earth-building practitioner.

Peter Hickson
Builder, Trainer, Consultant and Manager, Earth Building Solutions
President, Earth Building Association of Australia

# Contents

| | | |
|---|---|---|
| 1 | **Introduction** | 1 |
| | Straw & Clay - the potential and the possibilities | 1 |
| | Why straw and clay? | 1 |
| | Rendering & Plastering | 2 |
| | Sand Clay Renders | 2 |
| | Straw-Clay Renders | 2 |
| | Clay Paints | 4 |
| | Conclusion | 5 |
| 2 | **Preliminaries** | 7 |
| | Sourcing Materials | 7 |
| | Sourcing Clay | 7 |
| | Sourcing Sand | 9 |
| | Sourcing Straw | 10 |
| | Screens & Screening | 13 |
| | Testing Render Mixes | 16 |
| 3 | **Preparation, Application & Mixes** | 19 |
| | Wall Preparation | 19 |
| | Rendering onto previously painted walls or other really smooth surfaces | 20 |
| | Rendering onto Fresh Plasterboard | 20 |
| | Thick Render on Smooth Walls | 20 |
| | Rendering onto Rammed Earth and Compressed Earth Bricks | 21 |
| | Rendering onto Light Earth | 21 |
| | Rendering onto Mud Brick | 21 |
| | Rendering onto Cob | 22 |
| | Rendering onto Straw Bales | 22 |
| | Application Techniques | 23 |
| | The Mixes | 26 |
| | Clay Slip Mix | 26 |
| | Straw-Clay Render | 28 |
| | Straw Clay Mix | 30 |
| | Sand Clay Render | 34 |
| | Sand Clay Mix | 36 |
| | Clay Paint | 41 |
| | Wheat Paste Paint Mix | 42 |
| | Lime Casein Paint Mix | 42 |
| | Bi-carb Casein Paint Mix | 42 |
| | The Glues | 43 |
| | Wheat Paste | 43 |
| | Wheat Paste Mix | 44 |
| | Casein | 44 |
| | Casein Paint Mix | 45 |

| | | | |
|---|---|---|---|
| 3 | **Preparation, Application & Mixes Contd.** | | |
| | Linseed Oil | 45 | |
| | Reeds, Mesh & Nails | 46 | |
| | Mixing straw clay on a tarpaulin | 50 | |
| | Mixing render with a Larry hoe in a wheelbarrow | 52 | |
| | Mixing clay render in a concrete mixer | 53 | |
| | Mixing straw clay render with a rotary hoe | 55 | |
| | Mixing clay paint with a paint mixing drill | 57 | |
| 4 | **Tools for the Earth builder** | 61 | |
| | Hands | 62 | |
| | Sponge | 62 | |
| | Paint Brushes | 62 | |
| | Dustpan Brush | 63 | |
| | Wood Float | 63 | |
| | Poly Float | 64 | |
| | Hawk | 64 | |
| | Hard trowel | 64 | |
| | Flexible Trowel | 65 | |
| | Plastic Trowel | 65 | |
| | Inside Corner Trowel | 65 | |
| | Outside Corner Trowel | 65 | |
| | Curved Inside Corner Trowel | 66 | |
| | Putty Knife | 66 | |
| | Bread Knife | 66 | |
| | Fencing Pliers | 66 | |
| | Bale Needle | 67 | |
| | Bum Scrubber | 67 | |
| | Mud Brick Moulds | 67 | |
| | Tubs | 68 | |
| | Larry | 68 | |
| | Fork | 68 | |
| | Texture Gun | 68 | |
| | 18 Gauge Stapler | 69 | |
| | Paint Mixing Drill | 69 | |
| | Concrete Mixer | 69 | |
| | Rotary Hoe | 70 | |
| | Whipper Snipper | 70 | |
| | Shopping List of Tools for the Earth Builder | 71 | |
| | **References** | 72 | |

# 1. Introduction

The intention of this book is to have a detailed look at the painting and rendering of completed walls in new as well as in existing buildings. This will focus on sand-clay render, straw-clay render and clay paints.

All paints, plasters and renders are made up of a binder, a filler and a pigment. Modern paints and renders still have to follow this basic recipe. Now they use industrial and often toxic ingredients, while we will use local non-toxic ingredients.

## Straw & Clay - the potential and possibilities

Straw and clay can and have been combined in countless ways, providing housing for at least a third of the world's population since people started creating buildings.

## Why straw and clay?

If you have ever spent a night in a building constructed of clay and straw you would need no answer to that question.

Earthen buildings are alive, they breath, have no toxicity, block potentially damaging electromagnetic fields, are free of mould and maintain the humidity of the air at the perfect balance for human habitation. In addition, they heal and protect people.

It still amazes me that I can dig a hole, get a wheelbarrow of sub-soil, mix it with straw and create such a variety of products. These products can be used to build houses and other structures as well as creating beautiful natural finishes.

## Rendering & Plastering

Rendering or plastering is a craft as old as house building. The basic methods and concepts have changed little over time. The basic idea is to find a suitable material and to mix it with enough water so that it will stick to a wall. The render is applied with one's hands or a trowel and smoothed out. Once semi-dry or what is called 'leather hard', the wall is rubbed well to compress and toughen the finish.

## Sand Clay Renders

Sand clay renders are a combination of naturally sourced clays and sands. These are mixed together with water and sometimes a little straw to create a render.

Sand clay renders are typically applied with a hawk and trowel, but hands can also be used. Just like other types of render sand clay renders are applied, compressed and polished thereby creating beautiful and healthy natural finishes in new as well as existing buildings.

## Straw-Clay Renders

Until quite recently most light-earth and straw bale houses were rendered with sand based renders. This had serious limitations for the earth builder. The application techniques and the number of applications were derived from solid plastering methodologies. This consisted of three thin coats of render applied with a hawk and trowel. Each coat could only be 6mm to 10mm thick and had to dry before the next coat was applied over it.

The skills required to source, blend and apply these types of renders is fairly high. Not to mention the strain on the body. It is not surprising that rendering pumps became so popular with straw bale builders!

With the discovery of straw clay based renders by the authors of The Straw Bale House book, Bill & Athena Steen, the straw bale building game changed. A single thick coat of straw clay render is applied by hand and shaped into any form desired. This single coat is most often used as a base coat to protect and shape walls. Once dry a thin coat of sand clay render can go over the straw clay render if desired. Alternatively a straw clay render can become the final layer if it is compressed with a wood float when curing and polished with a trowel.

The type of clay you have, or can get is not as important in straw-clay render as it is in sand clay render. This is due to the high amount of straw in the mix.

The skills needed to apply straw clay render are easy to learn and the tools required are minimal. Most people quickly pick up the skill as though something inside them is rekindled from former lives.

Since I was taught straw-clay render I have used it on every project I have been involved with. It is so easy, so tough and so beautiful a render to apply and shape. Any odd hole or tricky spot that needs filling gets the straw-clay render treatment.

Straw clay can also be used for relief work, to shape window reveals, make built-in shelves and even benches. In my cob cottage I cast vaulted straw clay cabinets over a thin plywood formwork. Once the formwork was removed and the cabinet was dry I could stand on top of them!

## Clay Paints

Clay based paints are often used as the final coating on earth walls. Mud brick homes can be finished with clay paint alone, a process known as 'bagging' in Australia. Clay paints can also be used over earth render, plasterboard or other existing wall surfaces. Good quality properly finished render can eliminate the need to paint walls at all. Unfortunately walls generally get damaged during the construction process. Repairing such walls results in obvious joints or cold breaks. Painting the walls after repairs will make these joints far less visible. Even if a finished render is not damaged the colour may be wrong so the walls will get a paint job. After a few years the walls may also benefit from a fresh coat of paint.

The paints detailed in this book are clay based and glue stabilized. The glue used is either casein or wheat paste. There are other glue options available from companies specializing in earth building products. I have decided to focus on the easy home made versions of clay paint.

A coat of oil is the most basic way to preserve an earthen wall. Linseed oil alone is often used instead of a paint. This is because water and oil do not mix, so the oil can protect earth walls from water penetration.

## Conclusion

Clay paints, sand clay render and straw clay render are slightly different combinations of basic naturally derived products. The possible combinations are endless. The important thing to keep in mind is what are you trying to achieve and using the correct combination of materials to achieve those goals. Clay paint is merely a decorative thin layer that helps to protect the underlying render. This is often referred to as a sacrificial layer, similar to normal house paint. Sand clay

render is a little thicker, so it gives the building some protection. As sand clay render does not contain much fibre, its strength relies on good aggregate selection. Try to imagine a really miniature brick wall, with the sand being the bricks and the clay the mortar. Just like a brick wall sand clay render is great in compression but not so great in tension. So if the wall or building moves a crack will most likely occur. The straw clay render is so packed full of fibre that it is really good in tension, but not as good in compression as the sand clay render. Straw clay render is most often used over soft wall surfaces like straw bales or light earth to stiffen them up. The straw clay render resists cracking thus creating an ideal bridging surface between a soft wall and sand clay render.

Start experimenting with the gifts of sand, clay and straw. You will be amazed at what is possible.

# Part 2 Preliminaries

## Sourcing Materials

Modern industrial wall finishes such as plasterboard are available from most building suppliers around the world. Rather than apply lath and plaster to walls, nowadays sheets of plaster encased in paper are screwed in place and only the seams are plastered.

If you wish to move away from this industrial form of building and to create a natural clay and straw based building, getting supplies is not so convenient. You cannot just go to the store and get a box of pre-mixed straw clay render. So, what options do we have?

Firstly we need to get our hands on the materials used to make the renders. The three basic materials needed are sand, clay and straw. These products are available in most places around the world. Sometimes it takes a little bit of time to search them out. Other times the materials are on-site and just under

your feet. "As a general principle, it may be remarked that the walls of a cottage should always be built of the materials furnished by the soil or vicinity where it is situated."[1]

## Sourcing Clay

Clay is the binder or glue used in earthen construction. Clay exists everywhere on the planet in differing amounts. Clay is found in the subsoil, the soil layer under the fertile and crumbly topsoil. How deep down that is depends on the area. Many of the old gold mining towns in Australia have clay on the surface as the topsoil got destroyed in the

mad search for gold. Other areas the subsoil starts a spade depth or 300mm down, while others still there may be up to a meter of topsoil covering the subsoil. When digging a hole with a shovel it is normally quite easy to tell when you get to the subsoil. The colour of the earth normally changes and the earth gets noticeably harder.

The first and potentially easiest way to source clay is from the excavations required to build the building. Make sure that whoever is doing the excavation knows to place the topsoil in one pile and the sub-soil in another pile. The topsoil will be used to make your food gardens and all going well the sub-soil can be used for building.

Another option is to rent a backhoe or digger and dig the material yourself from your own land. Doing your own foundation excavations usually means that you need to rent the equipment anyway. Once you have cleared, graded and dug the foundations, dig a pond and do some landscaping. A little knowledge is needed to work out where to dig. Ask the old timers in your area what they think. Certain plants such as reeds and dock grow in areas with clay sub-soil.

Start by digging a small test hole and check that the sub-soil is suitable by following the tests described later in this chapter. If the tests are positive clear away the top soil first and save it for your food gardens, trying not to be too destructive. Try to make the hole as natural looking and beautiful as possible, piling the sub-soil in one spot. Always dig far more than you think you will need, as it will all get used. As you are digging on your own land it is highly possible that you will do a better job than a professional.

If the sub-soil removed from the excavations is not suitable, or it needs some amendments it is time to start looking around for sources of suitable alternative material. The easiest place to start looking is your local landscape and building suppliers. Call around and find out what they have in the way of sand or fill. Check out prices per meter and delivery costs. Then grab some bags or buckets and go to

the yard to get some samples. If your site soil is lacking in clay look for fill dirt or road base. These usually have a percentage of clay in them. The more samples you can get the better as each mix of sand and clay will behave differently. You never know what you have until you test it.

If you have no luck at your local landscape and building suppliers the next place to try is the local quarries or gravel pits, if you have any in your area. The material from these places should be cheaper than material from the landscape and building suppliers. Be prepared to buy a truckload, as that is what is usually required. Ring

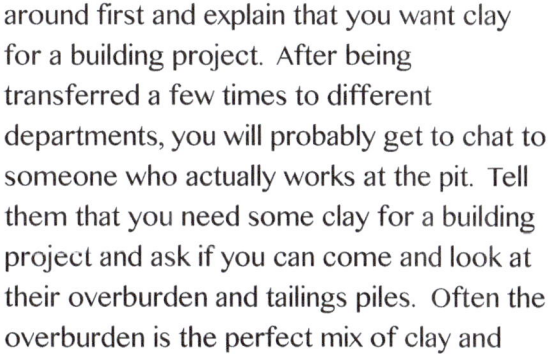

around first and explain that you want clay for a building project. After being transferred a few times to different departments, you will probably get to chat to someone who actually works at the pit. Tell them that you need some clay for a building project and ask if you can come and look at their overburden and tailings piles. Often the overburden is the perfect mix of clay and sand for rendering. You might get lots of roots and rocks mixed in with overburden, as it is the stuff they remove to get to the more pure deposits. Some quarries have clay for sale. Farmers buy it to seal ponds and councils use it to seal landfills.

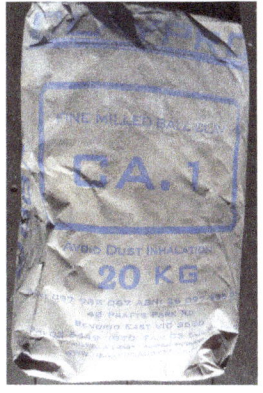

In large cities or towns it is often possible to get tuck loads of clay soil delivered for next to nothing. Ring around to all the local excavation companies and ask. You may have to pay a little for delivery, but usually the excavators are happy to get rid of it. The main problem is that you cannot check the quality or purity of the product you are getting. Many earthen structures have been built from free excavation waste so don't be shy! A carton of beer goes a long way towards building trust between earth builders and excavators!

Processed clay is available from most ceramic supply stores. The clay is a finely screened powder packaged into 20kg bags. There are often a few different types available. Kaolin is a nice white clay that makes fantastic render and paint. Fire clay will often have a yellow tint and also works well for renders and paint. Other earthenware or similar clays may also be available. As always test the materials before committing. These bagged clays can be expensive so are really only affordable for thin sand-clay render or clay paint.

## Sourcing Sand

The sand used in a render should be a mixture of various size grains. People will often refer to this type of sand as 'well graded aggregate'. The ideal render can be imagined as a puzzle with all the different sized sand pieces fitting neatly together. Sand is available from building and landscaping supply yards. There will normally be a few types to choose from and the choices, as well as the names of those choices will vary area to area. Most places will have a 'brickies' sand that is used to make brick mortar, a packing sand that is used under concrete slabs to create a firm base and a concrete sand that is used in making concrete. All yards will have sands available for these three basic functions. Often other sands will also be available.

As the brickies sand is used as a base for brick mortar it usually has uniform size aggregate of a small size. It will work with earthen plaster where strength is not required, so its best saved for finish work. Brickies sand usually has a percentage of clay in it. The colour of the clay and the amount of clay vary. Most yards have at least two types of brickies sand. Really nice finish renders can be made from brickies sand and a little wheat paste or casein glue. Sometimes no additions are needed.

Packing sand is used to fill in areas before pouring concrete. This sand usually has a good mixture of aggregate sizes from 6mm to 'fines' so it will pack down well. The actual mix will vary from place to place and even month to month. Often packing sand can be screened down to 3mm and be a fantastic premixed render.

Concrete sand is a mix of sand and small rocks used as a base for mixing concrete. It is a great sand to make cob or structural render with, you can also screen it down to 3mm for finer plasters. The differing sized aggregate will lock together and help to form a really strong render. It can be a fantastic sand for mixing cob, but usually requires lots of work to screen it down for render. Still if it is all you can get it will work and you can use the gravel left over for drainage.

Bagged sands are available from building and landscaping supply stores. The selection varies from place to place, so look around. As with all your materials play around with them, do lots of test patches and see what happens.

## Sourcing Straw

Straw had been used as an addition to mud bricks, cob and render for thousands of years. There are many good reasons for this. The straw fibres have been shown to provide added strength to earthen mixes. Often straw is used to stop cracking in bricks or render. This fact alone demonstrates the extra strength and support that straw gives to earth. Straw spread throughout a cob or render mix helps to tie the whole wall together into a fibrous mass.

Straw is the stem of grain producing crops.

Being the stem of the plant it is mostly made up of cellulose. Cellulose is the same material that wood is made out of. Hay on the other hand is the top part of various plants that has food value for livestock. The theory goes that if the material can be used to feed farm animals it can probably also feed smaller animals like rodents and bacteria. This is why we always use straw in our buildings. The type of straw used in construction is generally wheat, barley, oat or rice. Other straws can and have been used, as long as they are predominantly cellulose. Pea straw is great for mulch and compost because it breaks down quickly. This is not an attribute we want in our houses. Sugarcane mulch can be used in place of straw. I have found it to be as good as straw in many respects, just a lot stiffer. When buying straw you have a few choices of bale shape and size. There are straw bales that a person of reasonable fitness can lift and move around. There are also large round and square jumbo bales. These need heavy machinery to move around. Once a size is decided upon we need to inspect the bales for certain things. Firstly the smell of the bale is probably the most important issue. The bale should smell fresh, not musky or mouldy. Any hint of off smells could indicate the onset of decomposition. We want to build long lasting houses not compost, so if it smells wrong don't buy it. The next thing to look at is the seed content of the bales. Really good building bales have little to no seed in them. This normally requires the that farmer puts sheep in the paddock after the header has gone through. Once the sheep have eaten all the left over grain the stems can be baled. Farmers who specialize in producing straw bales for construction will often take this added precaution. The problem of having seed in straw that you are rendering with is twofold. Firstly anytime you introduce seed into a building you run the risk of attracting seed eating animals. Secondly the seeds can sprout while the render is drying out. This is not too much of a problem for base coat renders and actually looks really good. It does make clients a little nervous though. It is more of a problem for top coat renders as the sprouting seed makes a hole in the render when it dies and falls off. The only time it is OK to have seed in building bales is if you are building light earth walls. In that case the sprouting seed is beneficial as it helps to dry out the wall.

The last thing to look at when buying bales is how clean they are. Sometimes there can be lots of weeds in the bales and occasionally even dirt. While neither of these are too problematic in small occurrences, it does take time to separate them out from the straw.

Once the straw bales have been purchased and delivered to the site they have to be stored properly. It is no use to go and buy good quality bales and leave them exposed to the elements. Preferably straw should be stored inside a building on top of pallets. The pallets are important as they keep the bales off the ground, away from rising damp and condensation. If there is no inside space available a shipping container is a good option. They are easily hired or bought and double as a secure spot to store tools while building.

If you have no other option the straw bales can be stored outside, but you may sustain some losses. Being outside you must store the bales up on pallets. The bales should be stacked in such a way that rain can easily fall off them. Think of a pointy roofed house, rather than a flat topped terrace. The whole stack needs to be covered in at least two layers of black builders plastic. Plastic tarps will not keep your bales dry.

On and around the jobsite different terms are used when talking about straw. A bale is the way it comes from the farm with the strings still attached. A flake is a piece of the bale approximately 100mm thick, taken from a bale once it has been cut open. Loose straw is a flake that has been teased apart. Chopped straw is straw that has been put through a mulcher or chopped up with a whipper snipper in a barrel. Fine straw is chopped straw that has been put through a 6mm screen.

By varying the length and quantity of straw that we mix with clay and aggregate, the different earth building products are made. Even something as simple as straw clay render can be modified to serve different tasks by varying straw length and quantity in the mix. Chopped straw is used for the basic straw clay mix. Loose straw is used in high quantity to create sculptural elements. Fine straw is used in the mix to create relief work and a light weight render for doing overhead

work. Generally the more straw in the mix the higher the clay content needed to bind it together. As always test first to see the potential of your materials.

The interesting thing about adding straw to clay is the other beneficial effects gained. It has been long known in Japan that letting straw clay render sit for a year or two improves it. The improvements gained are more strength, higher water resistance, less cracking and more plasticity. To gain these beneficial effects a fermentation takes place between the straw and the clay. Other people like French natural builder Tom Riven have also used fermentation to improve the quality of straw clay render. He uses a starter made by soaking wheat or other plants in water for a few weeks to accelerate the fermentation process, rather than waiting for two years. In a similar process to making sourdough bread, a little of the starter is added to each batch of render. The render then sits over night before using.

Australian architect Allen Kong[2] did a study on the effects of straw in the production of mud bricks. He showed that adding straw did give the above stated benefits plus hardening promoted by material leached out of the straw. He also showed that by boiling straw in water and using the strained water to make bricks, that the same effects were seen. These bricks went super hard even without adding the straw at all.

I have found over the years that letting any render sit overnight definitely improves it. Often the day-to-day demands of building gets in the way. More often than not we just mix and apply the render the same day. Although not ideal I have noticed that in the thick applications of straw-clay render the fermentation seems to occur on the wall as the render is drying out. The characteristic smell lingers for about a week. A day or two after applying the render it seems to change and become harder to the point where it can be polished up like leather. For top coats of straw-clay render or sand-clay render that has some straw in it, letting the mix sit overnight will soften the straw. This helps to minimize those annoying poking out bits of straw that just don't seem to want to sit down in your render.

## Screens & Screening

The clay sub soil which we base all our earth building work around comes in many different forms. It is possible to strike it lucky and dig up some sub soil that's perfect to use straight away. It is also possible to buy clay that has been processed for you.

The sand we want to use may also need to be screened as well. Most brought in sand has some impurities such as bark, weeds or charcoal. To ensure a good clean consistent render it is best to screen them out. Often the sand we get delivered will be perfect for straw clay render, but need to be screened smaller for sand clay render. The screening and blending of sands and clays is the true art of the earth builder. The possibilities and beauty are endless. Most of the time we will end up doing some if not all of the processing ourselves. This is where screens come in.

A screen is simply a wooden frame with wire mesh attached to it. The material passes through the screen to achieve certain aims. The most common screen size is 6mm, that means the holes in the wire are 6mm across. Ideally the screen is made the size of a wheelbarrow. Then the sub soil or sand is passed through the screen into the wheelbarrow and everything 6mm or less will fall through

the screen while everything larger will stay on top. This 6mm subsoil makes a great base for straw clay render. For sand clay render the subsoil and sand is screened through a 3mm screen or a 1mm screen, depending on the desired thickness of the render. Theoretically the thinnest a render can be applied is twice the thickness of the screen size. This is the thickness of two of the largest pieces of sand sitting on top of each other. The maximum thickness a render should be applied is four times the screen size. After three times the thickness the aggregate size is too small to make a strong render and cracking or dusting may occur. So a 1mm screened render is applied at a minimum thickness of 2mm and a maximum thickness of 4mm. A 3mm screened render is applied at a minimum thickness of 6mm and maximum thickness of 12mm.

If the sand or subsoil is damp it may clog up the screen. In that case it pays to wait until the sub soil is dry or mix it with more water until a slurry is made. The slurry can

then be passed through the screen. This is easiest done with a concrete mixer making the slurry and a wheelbarrow with a screen over it waiting below. As with all things, it's an art and a science, so if it is too hard, you are doing something wrong!

Making the wooden frames for screens is fairly easy, finding the mesh to put on them can be a little tricky. The 6mm mesh can be bought easily at most larger hardware's or garden centres. It is sold as bird and mice wire. Finding the 3mm wire can be a little tricky, which is a shame as it is such a good size for sand clay renders. The 1mm wire is easy to find as it is sold as metal security door mesh. I have on occasion borrowed a fly screen off a window on the house I was working on to use as a 1mm screen.

When making paint it is best to find a stainless steel kitchen sieve that fits on a bucket and has a hole size of ½ a mm or less.

It is possible to go to even finer pottery screens. They are number graded - the higher the number the finer the grade.

Clay is the finest material on the planet, so the finer you screen things the more you concentrate the clay in your sample. Pure clay putties can be made by using these screens. Generally really fine clay is mixed with lots of water are run through the fine screen. This slurry is placed into a container lined with a sheet. The container should have holes in it so that the water can drain through the sheet and away from the clay putty. The putty can be stored damp or dried out for later use.

Straw can be screened through a 6mm screen for sand-clay and finish plasters - but it's slow going!

Once a sub soil is screened down I like to bag it up into 20 liter bags. This allows me to know what I have in stock and allows me to work out how much material I use per meter of render.

## Testing Render Mixes

Once a suitable sources of clay, sand and straw have been found it is time to do some testing. It is vital that you do numerous render test patches before proceeding with your project. Often the clay soil obtained is close to a useable mix.

Begin by screening some of the subsoil you want to test through a 3mm screen. If the sand you are going to use needs screening do that also.

Mix one cup of the screened subsoil with a little water and apply to a wall or a small piece of plasterboard with a trowel. A 300mm by 300mm sized square patch around 6mm thick is ideal. Next mix ½ a cup of the subsoil, ½ a cup of the sand and a little water together. Apply it next to the first sample with a trowel. Note down the proportions of subsoil and sand in each sample. Continue to increase the amount of sand by ½ a cup until you have 6 samples. This will give you test patches starting at 100% subsoil, to 1 part subsoil to 5 parts sand. It is likely that the 5 parts sand mix may not even stick to the wall! That is fine as we want to see the full spectrum of possibilities. When applying the samples try to note how they feel. Are they very sticky or sandy? This will give you clues for possible additions. Let the samples dry and see what happens.

Once dry some interesting things will have happened. If you have lots of clay in your clay soil the samples will have cracked lots. If you have lots of sand the sample may dust off and crumble really easily. Hopefully you have some cracking as this indicates a

good clay content. If so we can start to test for possible other additions to our render mixes.

Sand and straw are the two most commonly used additions. Both will achieve the desired results of stopping the cracking in the render. The straw clay render mix uses mostly straw, while the sand clay uses mostly sand. Often a combination of sand and straw makes the best mix.

Using the initial tests as a starting point, continue to test different possible render combinations. If more than one subsoil is available make sure to test each one individually and perhaps even try a blend. Try different sands in the mix to see what affect they have on the subsoil. The addition of straw to a sand clay mix should be tested at different amounts. Often by adding straw the amount of sand needs to be reduced. Straw can be added in a small amount as a purely decorative element or in a larger amount as a structural element. The more testing you can do the better the end results. Once happy with a mix it is wise to do a far larger test panel to see how the

render will work in the field. I have a 3 meter by 3 meter test wall with a window and a niche to test potential renders on. This test wall helps me to refine my rendering skills and shows me how easy or difficult it is going to be to render an entire house with the chosen mix.

These tests will only apply to the location you got the sub soil from. On my 5 acre property we had a large variation in sub soils. Some were almost pure clay, others almost pure silt. A friend 5 km down the road has sub-soil with the perfect combination of clay and sand/silt for render. Never make any assumptions about the sub soil you are using.

# Part 3 Preparation, Application & Mixes

## Wall Preparation

When deciding to render a wall with earth based materials the surface of the wall may or may not need some work before we can begin. Wall surfaces generally fall into two categories. The first is smooth walls. These walls already have the shape that we want and are ready for render. The second is rough walls. These walls need shaping, detailing and flattening. To achieve this the rough walls need a coat of straw clay render to shape them into the desired form. This coat should be at least 25mm thick to give strength and stability to the wall. Straw clay render is also often used to fill in depressions and to shape window reveals, even if the whole wall does not get covered with it. Once rough walls have received a coat of straw clay  render they become smooth walls. Rough walls include straw bale, light earth and earth bag walls. Smooth walls include plasterboard, previously rendered walls and rammed earth walls. Smooth walls may or may not need some extra preparation before receiving a sand clay render.

The wall type itself asks for different strategies to ensure a good long lasting bond. Below is my experience to date, I suggest you try the methods and proceed with caution. Always test things before committing and constantly ask yourself *what am I trying to achieve?*

All walls to be rendered must be treated properly to ensure a good bond. Any loose or flaking material should be scraped off. Cracks, holes and depressions should be filled, covered with gutter guard or mesh and allowed to dry. The entire wall should be solid and stable.

Depending on the substrate, different materials are used to treat and prepare the wall. The three choices I use are water, clay slip and glue. Unsealed raw earth walls have clay on them already so they only need to be misted with water to reactivate the existing clay before rendering.

Unsealed wall not created out of raw earth, like straw bale and earthbag walls, need to be sprayed with clay slip first to create a good bond. Previously sealed, painted or other really smooth walls need to be treated with glue. In this case the glue is mixed with sand, applied to the wall and allowed to dry.

## Rendering onto previously painted walls or other really smooth surfaces

When you find yourself faced with rendering previously painted walls or other really smooth surfaces an adhesion coat should be used. An adhesion coat is a thick paint-like glue with some sand in it. This is brushed or rolled onto the wall to provide a physical key or grip to the smooth surface. Once dry a coat of render that contains a little of the same glue in it is applied. Either wheat paste or casein glue can be used as the glue in the adhesion coat. Follow the recipe in the glue section [pages 42 & 45] and add some sand screened down to 1mm. It is important to keep stirring the mix while applying it to the wall as the sand always tries to drop out of suspension. We want a consistent spread of sand over the wall.

## Rendering onto fresh plasterboard

In new construction it is easier to add the sand to the plasterboard priming paint and use that as a combination sealer and adhesion coat. As the joint compound used with plasterboard is water sensitive, it is important to paint it with something that makes the joint compound water resistant. This is so that all the water in the render we apply does not reactivate the joint compound, possibly leading to failure.

Conventional plasterboard primer with sand works. Casein glue with sand will also do the job well. Wheat paste is not water resistant enough to trust to use over new plasterboard.

## Thick render on smooth walls

When a smooth wall wants a thick coat of straw clay render a better key or grip is needed than just an adhesion coat. This is to provide a physical key to make sure that the new render bonds to the wall. To provide the key a lath or mesh is needed. The use of earth based materials dictates staying away from metal lath or mesh as they can rust and cause failure. Reed mats are a good alternative that can be stapled to a wall. An adhesion coat should be painted on first. While still wet the reed mats should be stapled onto the wall with 18 gauge galvanised staples. Make sure the staples are going into the wood framing. Coat the reed mat with more of the adhesion coat and apply a straw clay render that has some glue in it straight away, working the render hard as it goes off will ensure a good bond. A top coat of straw clay or sand clay render can be easily applied once dry.

## Rendering onto Rammed Earth and Compressed earth bricks

Some raw earth walls are really smooth and hard. Rammed earth and Compressed Earth Brick walls need to be scratched up if you want to render them. Depending on the density of the wall this can be a tiring task. The idea is to create little 1mm to 3mm grooves every 50mm to 100mm horizontally on the wall. These little shelves give the backside of the new render little fins or keys that stick into the existing wall. An old flat head screwdriver or the point of a brickies trowel can be used to make the grooves. Sometimes the wall is so hard that a shovel or crowbar is needed. A clay slip coat should be used when rendering. A sand clay render, with or without straw is all that is needed on these smooth hard walls. Most people may question why you would render them at all.

## Rendering onto Light Earth

Light-earth or straw-clay is a combination of straw with just enough clay to stick the straw together. This material has been stuffed into the walls of houses for over 1000 years. To create a light earth building a structural timber frame is first constructed and the light-earth is tamped between temporary plywood forms. The forms are removed straight away and the walls are allowed to dry. Once dry they are rendered inside and out.

A light earth wall needs a nice thick layer of straw clay render to provide strength and shape to the walls. Water or clay slip is used to wet the walls prior to rendering. I tend to spray clay slip on to ensure a good bond. This is followed by 20mm of straw clay render and once dry 5mm of sand clay render. It is possible to apply 25mm of straw clay render and finish it off in one go if your mix is good.

## Rendering onto Mud Brick

The use of mud bricks in Australia is well known and loved. Unfortunately there has been a steady decline in their use with increasing energy standards. Most mud brick walls in Australia are finished by a process known as 'bagging'. Bagging is the application of a thickish paint with a paint brush or dustpan brush. Traditionally, once slightly dry the paint is rubbed with a bag , a sponge or a wet brush to smooth it out. Really old mud brick houses in Australia are rendered inside and out so that they look like any other masonry building. I have seen two examples from the late 1800's. These were mostly rendered with river silt. As time and environmental ethics progressed the use of river silts has subsided. It is still possible to render a mud brick building with earthen render using clay subsoils, rather than river silt.

Water is sprayed onto the wall to wet it down and either a sand clay or straw clay render goes straight on. Sand clay is used if the look of the bricks is to be maintained. Straw clay render is used to flatten the walls and shape window reveals if so desired.

## Rendering onto Cob

Cob walls are built by hand without the use of formwork. Cob is really an earthen concrete with some long straw for reinforcement. The large amount of aggregate it contains means it does not shrink much on drying. This gives cob amazing sculptural possibilities. When the walls are drying they are trimmed back with a shovel to the exact shape desired. This creates a perfect surface for render. Water is used to wet the walls and then a coat of sand clay render is applied. Straw clay render is often used to shape window reveals and create the other decorative details that cob homes are famous for.

## Rendering onto Straw Bales

With the steady increase of energy efficiency standards in Australia over the last few decades the use of straw bales in the construction of homes has been on the increase. Straw bale homes have many advantages and certain idiosyncrasies. The use of clay renders on straw bales homes (at least internally) is critical to there longevity. Clay is so much more moisture loving than the straw that it constantly pulls moisture out of

the inside of the walls and keeps the straw preserved. The straw is wet with a clay slip coat just prior to applying a coat of straw clay render. How much render is needed depends on the amount of preparation done to the straw bales prior to rendering. I would not like less than 25mm of straw clay render over the bales. As the straw clay render is so thick it will not go off too quickly so we can keep topping up bits here and there for the next day or two. The straw clay render can be finished off if your mix is really good or a coat of sand clay render can go over the top.

Most straw bale houses are rendered externally in Australia with a lime sand render for ease of maintenance.

## Application Techniques

The clay based renders in this book require the same basic process in application.

Apply ➡ Compress ➡ Polish

Apply the render with your hand or trowel to the wall. Wait 10 to 60 minutes, depending on mix, climate, weather and substrate.

Compress render with a wood or poly float using a circular motion.

Wait 10 to 30 minutes, depending on mix, climate and weather.

Polish the render with a flexible stainless steel or a plastic trowel.

This combination of apply, compress and polish is what will make durable, dust and crack free render.

When render is first applied it has lots of water in it. As the render dries out the water that was in the render leaves and the spaces where the water was in the render are now tiny air pockets. Compression closes up these air pockets and smoothes out the shape of your wall. During compression new material can be added to fill in imperfections.

Polishing smoothes the render and makes a hard surface. Just like finishing a concrete slab, polishing brings some of the 'milk' to the surface. This milk fills in any pin holes or cracks. Water can be misted onto the wall while polishing to increase the amount of available milk.

The choice of trowel, timing and technique will all have an effect on the finished look of your render. With a little research and a lot of experimentation anything is possible.

## The Mixes

## Clay Slip Mix

Clay slip is water mixed with clay to make a paint like liquid clay. It is used as the glue and primer for earthen construction.

Clay slip is applied as a primer coat before rendering. It should be applied a small section at a time just prior to applying the render. If the clay slip on the section of wall you are rendering dries out before you render over it, apply more.

Clay slip is used to make light earth and can be used as a base to make the renders with. Some earth builders only mix their renders from clay slip and never from dry materials. This produces a higher quality end product as the clay has had time to rehydrate. It is believed that the hydration or soaking allows the clay to get into full suspension in the water. Once dry a stronger and harder end result is achieved.

To make clay slip mix clay and water together until it achieves a smooth and slightly thick consistency. To test if you have a decent clay slip, stick your finger in it. The slip should stick to your finger and totally cover the fingerprint, as if you had stuck your finger in a pail of paint.

If you want to make clay slip from dry subsoil, firstly screen it down to 6mm. You can alternatively also use a bagged clay which is already screened. Fill a container ¾ full with water, add the dry clay and mix well. A large drill with a paint mixer bit works well for this. Test the thickness of the slip using the finger method. Silt and sand do not stick to your finger, clay does. Once the skin on your finger is totally covered with the slip it is done.

If you are starting with a damp clay, mix the clay with water as best you can and screen the mix through a 6mm screen. If the clay still does not screen, mix it up some more and let sit overnight. By morning the clay should have softened enough to screen. Some clays will never really soften in water. They need to be smashed up mechanically before use.

All clay slip will work better if left for a few hours or even overnight. This resting period settles out the heavy aggregates and brings the water to the surface.

In most situations we just give the slip a quick mix before use. If the available subsoil is very low in clay, the next morning the water is carefully poured off and the slip harvested. This is done by scooping the top layer out off the bucket and dodging the aggregate at the bottom. A fairly pure clay slip can be produced in this way from almost any sub-soil.

For bulk production a wheelbarrow should have subsoil constantly soaking in it. When more slip is required the wet clay is taken from the wheelbarrow, mixed with a hoe or a heavy duty drill and then screened. The wheelbarrow is then filled back up with clay and water. It is possible to always have bulk clay slip on hand using this method.

Clay slip can be applied to straw and earthen walls in a few different ways.

• Hand application is a messy business. Mixing in a little finely cut straw will help. A thick slip is required for hand application.

• Brushing onto the wall with a broom head or dustpan brush is a little cleaner. Experiment with different brush types until you find one that works for you.

• Spraying clay slip is normally done through a texture gun. This is definitely the most effective method to get the slip deep into straw bales.

## Straw-Clay Render

Straw-clay render is a marvel of modern earth building. It was discovered by Bill & Athena Steen[3] whilst working in Mexico. Not being able to get a delivery of sand to render the straw bale building they were working on dictated a render of clay and straw alone. The locals they were working with suggested using the light earth mix they had been making bricks out of as a render. By adding a little more clay to the light earth mix and using shorter straw, straw-clay render was born.

Being so full of fibre the straw-clay render is incredibly strong, yet flexible. It is just like an earthen fibreglass. Straw-clay render is a

perfect combination for straw bale construction. Its combined strength and flexibility are unmatched by lime or cement finishes. It is very breathable, easily repairable, more water resistant than other clay based renders, can bridge over timbers and is highly sculptural.

Interestingly, in Japan a similar mix called Aratsuchi Daub has been used for centuries as the base coat in the Japanese version of wattle & daub. Subsoil and rice straw are mixed together with feet and garden forks. This is done in a pit lined with plastic. Once mixed the Aratsuchi Daub is left to sit for up to two years. Ron Edwards briefly describes a mix of subsoil and straw being used as a render in China on cave and mud brick buildings. Once mixed the mud would be left to sit for a few hours before application. (R.Edwards 1984)[4]

I guess that such a basic and useful mix has probably always been used around the world by earth builders.

The basic mix and concept of straw-clay render are easily learnt. Basically you mix enough clay with water until it is as thick as cream. Then stick your finger in it. The clay slip should stick to your finger and cover it completely, just like if you stuck your finger in a can of paint. If the clay slip you just made does not completely cover your

finger add more clay, or your sub-soil may not have enough clay in it. When it is thick enough add lots of straw until a sticky yet workable mix is achieved. This will require more straw than you imagine. The final mix will be sticky enough to stick to any surface. Sand may be required in the mix if the render cracks too much or it is being applied as a single coat. Adding sand will also bring in more strength to a subsoil that does not have much naturally occurring sand in it.

## Straw Clay Mix

2 parts clay @ 6mm
1 part sand
1/2 part straw @ 20 to 50mm

2 parts clay @ 6mm
1/2 part straw @ 20 to 50mm

1 part clay @ 6mm
1 part sand
½ part straw @ 20 to 50mm

It is obvious by the proportions of materials in the recipes above that the exact mixture is an art as much as a science. The final mix should be relatively easy to apply to a wall. If it is too dry you will tire very quickly.

If the straw clay is not sticking easily to the wall, your mix is too wet or you need more clay in the mix. Often, applying a clay slip to the surface first will help. Always wet the wall first with either water or clay slip.

To apply, grab a handful of the straw clay render in one hand and a wooden float in the other hand. Squish the plaster render on the wall in an upwards movement and smooth it out with a wooden float. Shape your wall with a wooden float until it is looking roughly like what you want. Then let the wall sit for 1 to 3 hours and go over it again with the wooden float. This will start the compression. As the render is so thick it may need to sit for up to 12 hours before compression.

You can tell when it is time to compress the render when the clean wet wood float only moves around the top 1mm of render. If more than the top 1mm of the render moves around it is too wet to compress. Try a few different areas on the wall as drying times can vary a lot on walls that were not flat prior to rendering. Sometimes due to the weather or substrate you may just have to wait longer. The noise of the wood float grinding the render is a good indication of the correct time for compression. When it is still too wet the moisture in the render makes the float

slip, rather than grind. This slippage does not really produce a sound. The dry grinding process produces a recognisable sound.

There is a real sweet spot in compression. Do it at the right time and your wall will smooth out quite easily. Wait too long and it is an arm breaker. If it has gone too hard you can mist the wall to re-hydrate it. This is best done by misting until water starts to flow down the surface, then stop and wait for 5 minutes. Mist a second time until the water starts to flow down the surface and stop for another 5 minutes. Mist for a third time and the top 1 to 2mm of render should be able to be worked. The trick is to allow the clay to soak up water slowly, if you try to do it too quickly the plaster will not become re-workable. Otherwise, it's best to just leave it and to apply another coat of render over the top.

To compress, a wet wooden float is used in backwards and forwards arcs, in combination with circular movements on the wall. It can take a little bit of pushing so two hands on the float is ideal, one on the handle and the other just in front of the handle on the wood. This hand position gives far better compression and less body fatigue. Keep the float clean and wet by dipping it in a bucket of water and wiping off the clay build up.

The amount you compress the wall is up to you. It is possible to keep working straw clay render until it is dry. Eventually a very hard almost leather like surface is achieved. For most applications a quick once over is all that is needed.

If another coat of render or paint is going over the straw-clay, just compress it until it looks good like what you want. You can keep adding bits here and there over the next few days and add relief if desired. This allows us to really get the building looking like what you want. Alternatively, the straw clay render can be polished up.

A flexible stainless steel or plastic trowel is best for polishing. Once again timing is everything. Get it right and a little bit of milky moisture will come to the surface. The render itself should not move at all. This 'milk' gets polished in to the surface to fill in imperfections and harden the finish. Wait too long and you get no milk and no polishing. A light sponging or misting can help to bring up the milk. The sponge can also bring up straw, which is hard to get to sit down again.

If the wall is too dry when it comes time to polish it, or full of cracks and you still want to polish, there is one last option.

Mix up some very fine clay with a little water and screen it through a kitchen strainer (usually 1/2mm). Scrape the mix onto the wall with a hard trowel, riding the edge. You do not want to add a new surface coating, just fill in the imperfections and cracks. Scrape the mix off with the hard edge of the trowel. This process should stimulate bringing up the milk and mix it with your new fake milk. The finished result will never look as good as a wall done properly, but most people will probably never notice. Another way to fix a cracked or damaged wall is to re-hydrate it. To re-hydrate a clay wall the wall is misted 3 times with a 5 minute rest in between each misting. During the third misting a sponge or sponge float is used in conjunction with the mister to smooth out the top 1 to 2mm of render.

Rounded corners and edges should be polished with a piece of plastic dipped in water. The plastic has to be fairly thick, yet still flexible. Packaging plastic waste lying around job sites often works great. Some people put rags in the plastic and tie it off in a tennis ball shape. Interior rounded corners can be shaped with a piece of plastic pipe with a drawer handle screwed onto it. A second slightly smaller piece of pipe with a handle, is used later on to finish the wall.

Depending on the desired use and finished product, the basic straw clay render mix can be altered. If the mix is being used as a rough base coat or for roughing in sculptural elements, try to make a mix containing lots of sticky clay, a small amount of sand and lots of straw. This mix will stick to anything due to the light weight and stickiness of the clay, it will even stick upside down. It is light enough to be moulded into almost any shape. It will most likely crack on drying due to the high clay content. As long as those cracks are non structural, this is not a problem. A structural crack is one where the render either side of the crack moves when tapped with a finger. This is a sign of the render not properly sticking to the wall surface. No movement when tapped shows that the render has bonded properly and the cracking is not a concern.

If the desire is to apply and polish the straw clay render all at one time, the mix becomes far more critical and the process more demanding. A medium clay content mix with lots of sand and a medium amount of straw is needed. The problem we may run into with this mix is a lack of stickiness for application. The lower clay content means less bonding. Different clays react differently, so, testing is critical to achieving a crack and dust free finish. Most the time even after testing you will get the mix pretty close and be happy with the finish. A coat of oil, wheat paste or casein will finish off the job perfectly. Sometimes you will hit the sweet spot - it all depends on the sub soil, testing and technique.

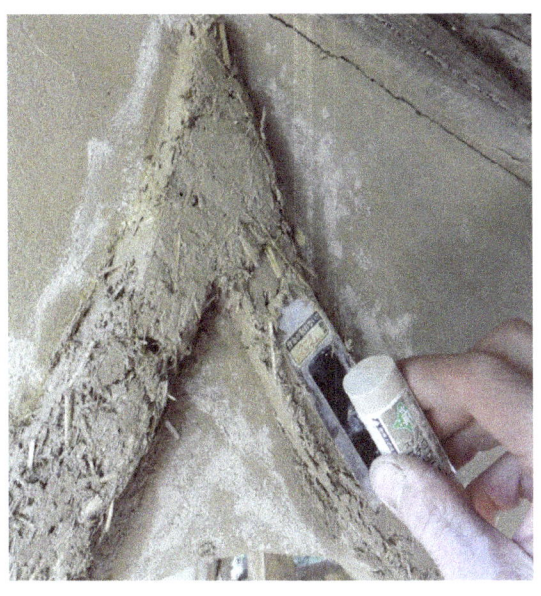

For relief work or detailed sculpture a finer mix is needed. A mix with a high amount of clay and shredded straw usually works. Screen the clay down to 3mm. Chop the straw up with a whipper snipper and then screen the chopped straw through a 6mm screen. This mix will be super light and sticky, not at all like a normal render. It is used to rough shape relief and sculpture with. It also comes in handy as a filler when repairing mud brick houses. Once dry a sand clay render will go over the top to smooth it out.

Mixing the straw-clay render ahead of time will improve the mix. It will not go bad, it will improve as the straw ferments and releases its organic admixture-like effects. The toughness and waterproofness of the render will be improved. Even just letting the render sit overnight will help soften the straw and give some of the admixture type effect. The smell will increase as the

mixture improves. This is not a problem for external plasters as the smell dissipates and the improved hardness / waterproofness is appreciated. Indoors though the smell can take up to 4 weeks to disperse. The Japanese Aratsuci Daub is allowed to sit for a minimum of one week, although two years is believed to be ideal. (E.Reynolds 2009)[5]

## Sand Clay Render

Sand clay render is the most basic, the most varied and in my opinion the most beautiful of the earthen renders. Possibly the earliest form of render made by people after they realized that the earth can be blended in varied ways to make it work better as a render. By adding some sand to sub soil the amount of cracking can be eliminated. Add too much sand and the render will become weak and

dusty. There are so many options when it comes to choosing sands and clay, that the finished look is infinite. By blending different coloured sands with different clays it is possible to create almost any look. For me the real beauty in this plaster is in the way that from a distance the wall looks like it is just one colour. Then something catches your eye, a bit of straw or different coloured aggregate. So you walk over for a closer look. Up close the nature and components of the render reveal themselves. You can often see the different coloured sands, clays and miniature pieces of rock that came from the sub soil. The amount and length of straw used in the mix can radically change the finished appearance. Such depth and variety is a celebration of earth building and of the earth itself.

Clay sub soil found on site or a clay imported from a known source is screened through a 3mm screen. The 3mm minus size produced is a fantastic aggregate size for sand clay render. Using the rule of thumb that the largest piece of aggregate should be half as thick as the render, 3mm allows us to apply 6mm to 10mm of render in each application. This thickness of render gives us the scope to work the render properly through all the stages of application, compression and polishing. Any thinner and the render may dry too quickly to compress. In that situation we just go straight to the polishing stage and use a plastic trowel to compress and polish at the same time. A better result occurs if all the stages are followed. To start with the render is applied with a hard steel trowel to the wall. After a period of drying the surface is compressed to push down the larger aggregate and bring up the milk, then the milk is polished into a shiny surface. This process is a traditional rendering process.

A concrete mixer or paint mixing drill is used to mix the sand clay render. Often finely chopped straw is added to bring in extra strength and visual interest. It all depends on what you are trying to achieve. A sand clay colour coat is blended from specific sands and clays to achieve a certain colour. Often kaolin clay is used as a base for adding pigment to due to its nice white colour and good workability. If the render is used as a straightening coat over cob or mud bricks, a thicker mix with finely chopped straw is used.

The addition of finely chopped straw has many advantages, but can be problematic if not allowed to soften. Little bits will stick up here and there, sometimes pulling away parts of the render during polishing. Letting the render sit for a day before application will soften the straw and bring in the special admixture effects to the render.

It is possible to select specific coloured sands, rock or even shell grit to put into the render. This material can be exposed before polishing just like producing an exposed aggregate concrete slab. The options are as endless as your imagination. When searching around for rendering material grab samples of anything that has some clay in it. Often you will see evidence of cracking in dry parts of the material, or cracking on the ground adjacent to the pile of material. Road base, quartz driveway mix and packing sand often are perfect sand clay render when screened down to 3mm. If possible test all your local options so that you have a steady supply of materials with known behaviours.

Sand clay render is usually applied with a hawk and trowel. A stiff trowel is used for application, later a more flexible one is used to polish. After application a wooden or poly float is used to compress and flatten.

### Sand Clay Mix
1 clay @ 3mm
2 sand
1/4 straw @ 0mm to 12mm

1 clay @ 3mm
3 sand

To make sand clay render mix the sub soil that has been screened down to 3mm with enough sand to prevent cracking upon drying. How much sand is needed and what type of sand is best is found by testing. The render should easily stick to the wall, if not something is wrong. Too much water can cause the render to loose its binding ability. Too much sand or not enough clay are other potential problems. Working out the best

combination of materials for a sand clay render is more like a treasure hunt than a job. Four issues present themselves when blending sand clay render; smoothness of finish, cracking, dusting and colour. Of the four issues the first three can be handled, the fourth is problematic.

Smoothness of finish is all about aggregate. A smooth render needs a well graded aggregate with enough fines to fill in all the voids and enough clay to rise a cream. The sub soil that is used to create sand clay render is a naturally occurring blend of clay, sand and silts. Testing is needed to work out the perfect aggregate combination. Some sub soils need lots of fine sand added to them to make a smooth render. Other sub soils need a course sand added to bring strength to a really smooth render.

Cracking is due to too much clay and conversely dusting is due to too little clay. There is a real sweet spot in all sub soils where the finished render does not crack or dust. Some sub soils have quite a large sweet spot, while other have a very narrow one. Generally the closer the mix is to cracking, but just not cracking, the better and stronger the render. Proper application techniques can get a render that wants to crack, finished perfectly!

The problem with the fourth issue is that it is possible to blend any colour imaginable with white clay, white sand and pigment. The problem is getting the client to like it after application. Many a fine render job has turned sour due to peoples different appreciation of colour. To overcome this some earth builders render it smooth and leave the paint job to the clients.

Timing is everything in applying and finishing sand clay render. The straw clay base coat or other wall surface should be completely dry. Mask off the ceilings and surrounding walls 10mm to 15mm wider than the wall to be rendered. Mask windows if they have been installed and put drop sheets on the floor. The application process can be a little messy, especially if the mix is a little wet.

Apply the sand clay render with a hard steel trowel, misting the wall first with water to slow down the drying process. Start at the top of the wall and fill in the whole top edge. On large walls two to three people may have to work together to get the wall finished in one go. It is best to do the whole wall corner to corner at one time, as it is extremely difficult to conceal stopping points.

As you work down the wall fill in the sides first, like a picture frame. Then fill in the field or middle of the wall. When a window or door is in the wall it is good to fill up the reveals all the way around the window first, before starting the wall. The reveals usually require more render to obtain the required shape, so doing them first gives them a little more time to dry. Ideally this will allow the whole wall to be compressed and polished at the same time. When working as a team one person can be starting on the window or door while the other person is starting at the ceiling. Once the window or door is done the two of you can fill in the rest of the flat parts of the wall together.

Usually, after a wall is finished it is time to smooth it out. If not, wait approx 30 minutes until the render can be compressed with a wood or poly float. The float should roughen up the surface off the wall as it compresses it. Areas that are not looking rough are low spots. This is the time to fill them in with a little more render until the whole wall has an even roughness. Do not worry too much now about the smoothness of the wall, all you are trying to do is push down the large aggregate and get an even surface. The polishing stage will smooth everything out for you.

Wait about another 30 minutes and polish with a flexible steel or plastic trowel. The trowel is used in a combination of circular motions and side to side motions. Only the top 1mm of render should be moving around at this stage. Move to a different spot or wait longer if more than the top 1mm is moving. It should be possible to bring up a little cream from the render. This cream is used to fill in pin prick holes and any hairline cracks that have appeared. The sound of the trowel working on the wall is a great indication of dryness and smoothness. Rough sandy sounding trowel strokes mean rough render, smooth sounding trowel strokes mean smooth render.

If the plaster has dried out too much to polish you can mist it with a little water or sponge the wall. A bucket of clean water is kept on hand with a sponge in it. The sponge is ringed out almost dry and wiped in circular motion on the wall. The flexible trowel then smooths the surface out. The sponge should be just damp, not so wet that water is running down the wall.

When polishing I like to go over the whole wall first and then focus in on the windows. Often the window reveals will need a little topping up. How far you go with the polishing process depends on the required look and the disposition of the renderer. Once the wall is almost dry a soft natural bristled dustpan broom is used to remove any surface sand and provide a final polishing. A firm, arched, left to right motion is used. The time to broom is just before the wall is totally dry. The broom should not leave marks on the wall. This final process can really toughen up the render, to a point where no paint is required.

Alternatively, skip the polishing and smooth the plaster out with a damp sponge. Soft circular motions with the sponge works best. Keep rinsing the sponge in a bucket of water as you go. A fairly high level of finish can be achieved with a sponge.

Sand-clay plaster should be fairly dust free without any additions. Often people want the look of earth with the durability of plastic. In that case a little help from wheat paste, casein or one of the commercially available admixtures can be added. Clay paint, wheat paste, casein or linseed oil can also be painted on afterwards.

## Clay Paint

Paints are the final coating used on most walls. Linseed oil alone is often used instead of paint. Clay based paints can be simple and made at home or they can be as complex as some of the imported zero VOC paints available on the market.

Good quality properly finished render can eliminate the need to paint walls at all. Unfortunately walls generally get damaged during the construction process. Repairing such walls results in obvious joints or cold breaks. Painting the walls after repairs will make these joints far less visible.

Even if a finished render is not damaged the colour may be wrong so the walls will get a paint job. After a few years the walls may also benefit from a fresh coat of paint.

The clay paints detailed in this book are clay based and glue stabilized. The glue used is either casein or wheat paste. To the glue base we add pigment, fine sand, fine clay and enough water to thin it down to a paint like consistency. Everything is mixed up well and brushed onto the wall. It is possible to use a roller to apply if the sand and clay is screened down enough or talc is used instead of sand. Otherwise a paint brush or dust pan brush is used to apply the paint. This paint is often used as the colour coat that goes over the earthen and plaster board walls in a house, to blend everything together.

The colour of the paint can come from the colour of the clay or a pigment. I tend to use the same clay as was used in the render as a base for the paint, unless a different colour is desired. Using the same clay allows me to put a protective layer of paint over the wall without changing the colour or look of the previously applied render.

If a different colour is wanted a white clay is used and pigment is added to the water and glue. The colour will have to be tested and a strict recipe followed to maintain consistency. Weighing the amount of pigment with a digital scale is the only way to maintain consistency. Often it is better to mix up a large batch, rather than lots of small ones to assure consistency of colour. You can buy concrete oxides to use as pigment and they are non-toxic, if you stay away from the greens and blues. If you really want greens and blues track down Sinopia or Kremer pigments. Both companies offer a large range of non-toxic pigments.

To make the paint, gather all the ingredients and a large bucket. If you are using pigment start by mixing it into the water with a paint mixer on a drill. Once the pigment has been well blended into the water, add the glue and mix with a big drill. Follow the recipes below for the glues. The wheat paste needs to be cooked before it can be added. The Casein glues are just added to the bucket dry and mixed in. I like to add the clay next and mix the whole lot up until the clay seems to be thoroughly mixed. It is easiest to buy bagged clay from ceramic suppliers to make this paint. Otherwise screen down your site clay to 1mm.

The sand or talc is then added and the paint is given a final mix.

Screen the paint into a second bucket through a 1mm or finer screen. The cheap stainless steel kitchen sieves are ideal for this and it is possible to get some really fine ones if you shop around.

Test the thickness of the paint to see if it needs a little more water and another quick stir up. Make sure you are keeping accurate notes of the exact mixture for future reference, especially if you have used a pigment.

Wheat Paste Paint Mix:
1 cup flour cooked with 3 cups water
6 extra cups water
2 to 4 cups 1mm or finer clay
0 to 2 cups fine sand or talc

Lime Casein Paint Mix:
1 cup skim milk powder added to 8 cups water
1 cup lime
1 cup 1mm or finer clay
0 to 1 cup fine sand or talc

Bi-carb Casein Paint Mix:
1 cup skim milk powder added to 8 cups water
6 Tbsp Bi-carb soda
2 to 4 cups 1mm or finer clay
0 to 1 cup fine sand or talc

A good recipe to start with is 1 part sand and 1 part clay. It can be possible to use 100% clay, it all depends on the clay.

Depending on the desired use of the paint different sized clay and sand can be selected. If a thick paint is desired to smooth out a mud brick wall before a second finer paint is applied, 3mm sand can be used. The larger sand grains will help to fill in the voids and cracks in the wall. Then a 1mm sand or talc can be used in the second coat to make a really smooth finish.

As the glue is doing most of the work binding the paint to the surface, we do not wet the wall before applying our clay paint. Use a paintbrush, roller or dustpan brush to apply. It takes a little experimentation to find the type of brush that works for you. Different situations will call for different brushes.

Start at the top of the wall and work down to avoid spilling stuff on your completed section. Wait a little while and smooth out brush strokes with a slightly moistened paintbrush / dustpan brush. Alternatively a sponge can be used in light circular motions to compress. Keep rinsing the sponge in a bucket of water. Once happy with the look of your wall, you're done!

## The Glues

As the glues used in the clay paints are derived from food products they are prone to spoiling. It is best to mix and apply the paint the same day. This is the main reason that these paints fell out of favour with commercial painters. Once acrylic paint was developed and the left over's could be stored for a very long time, the natural paints fell by the wayside.

## Wheat Paste

Wheat paste is a natural starch based glue made by heating a mixture of flour and water. This glue can be derived from wheat, rye or rice flour. It is commonly referred to as wheat paste in natural building circles as wheat flour is most commonly used. It is also called wall paper paste and clag.

Wheat paste increases the hardness and stickiness of clay renders plasters while reducing the dustiness. It gives little or no water resistance, so is generally only used as an addition to interior plasters and paints.

Wheat paste can be used to install wallpaper as well as being used in paints and as an additive to clay based plasters. It is possible to make a very strong plaster from wheat paste and sand alone. I tend to use organic flour, white or wholemeal to make wheat paste as that is what I usually have around. Most people use cheap white flour. Once made the wheat paste does need to be used that day as it tends to spoil quickly.

### Wheat Paste Mix:

1 cup flour

3 cups water

Whisk together 1½ cups water with 1 cup flour. Bring ½ cup of water to the boil on a stove. When boiling, pour in the floured water and whisk like mad until it thickens up. Turn off the heat before it burns.

Mix 1 part wheat paster with 2 parts water to make the base for paint or finish plaster. If your wheat paste turns out lumpy, screen it before use.

### Casein

Casein is a binder made from milk protein. Before acrylic paints were freely available Milk or Casein paints were widely used.

To make casein paint the milk protein is mixed with lime. This produces a chemical reaction that forms calcium albuminate, a wash-resistant compound. (G.Minke 2009)[6]

Bi-carbonate of soda or baking soda can also be used to create casein. The lime-casein is a stronger binder than the bi-carb-casein.

For interior paints I usually use the bi-carb version as it is easy to make and does change the colour of the paint as much as the lime version which makes everything white.

Casein can be used to strengthen finish coat renders. I mainly use it as a base for clay paints.

Skim milk powder is a cheap and easy way to get milk protein. Other methods can be used as a little internet research will reveal. The skim milk powder is mixed with water and the bi-carb or lime is added. This is mixed again and a slight frothing should occur. The frothing indicates that the casein binder is being formed - no froth no good!

The casein base can now be added to renders or paints. Some type of filler is needed for paint as the casein is quite thin. Clay and talc are the most commonly used fillers.

## Casein Paint Mix:
1 cup skim milk powder
8 cups water
6 Tbsp Bi-carb soda or 1 cup Lime
Mix the milk powder with the water first.
Add Lime or Bi-carb soda and mix again.

## Linseed Oil

Linseed oil has a long and proud history as a preservation tool. The first paints were linseed oil mixed with pigment and a filler. A coat of linseed oil is the most basic way to preserve an earthen wall. Many of us have used linseed oil on cricket bats or mixed it with turpentine before applying it to wood.

The linseed oil we want to use in all our building and plastering work is sun thickened raw linseed oil - not boiled linseed oil. Boiled linseed oil is not really boiled - it is heated gently to remove oxygen and then combined with metal salts like cobalt and driers that have suspect negative health effects. Sun thickening achieves the same aim of helping the oil to dry more quickly. Essentially, we pre-set the oil by exposing it to the air.

The sun thickening of raw linseed oil is an ancient art. The oil is placed in a tub in direct daylight with a glass cover for 6 to 8 weeks. Air must be able to get into the oil and once every so often it should be stirred.

Over the 6 to 8 weeks the rancid smell of the raw oil will have gone and the colour will be milky yellow to clear. If you leave a drop on a plate overnight a skin would have formed on top of the drop of oil. The oil has been pre-dried.

If you want totally clear oil, mix it with equal parts water and wait for the water and oil to separate. Next, freeze the water and pour off the clean oil. You will have to do this a few times to get a totally clear oil.

Paint the thickened oil onto clay plasters. Externally, the protection will fade over 12 or so months if exposed to direct sunlight. The oil will last far longer indoors or under a roofline.

Mix 1 part oil with 1 part citrus thinners or gum turpentine to make a wood preservative.

Add some talc or chalk and a little pigment to create an oil paint.

It is important to note that sun thickened linseed oil will darken the clay based plaster a fair amount, so always do some tests before use.

## Reeds, Mesh & Nails

Render relies on a solid substrate for strength. If the material the render is applied onto moves or shrinks, the render will probably crack. Most often this occurs when render bridges over timber as over time the timber shrinks, pulling away from the render. Bridging render over metal is even more difficult as metal expands and contracts with heating and cooling.

Many different approaches have been used to solve this issue. Usually a combination of fibre in the render mix and some sort of mesh covering the timber does the job. Metal needs some extra covering to allow it to expand and contract without cracking the hard render coating. Wrapping the metal in hessian or rags gives a buffer between the metal and the render. Always remember to cover the whole area with a mesh as well. On lime rendered buildings metal render mesh is normally used. However, since clay and metal are not very compatible, other products are used.

Reed mats or Euro reeds have been used successfully with clay and lime renders for many years in the USA and UK. I first encountered them in the USA. They are a quick-growing water reed tied together with light wire. Usually sold in 1.8 by 3m bundles for around $20, they cost lots less than metal render mesh. The nice thing about reed mats is that they are easy to cut up and shape. They don't cut your hands to shreds like render mesh either. The reeds can be used to shape window reveals, to cover large expanses of timber and to fill the space between the top bale and the ceiling.

To attach the reed to bales, metal pins are used. To attach the reeds to timber, staples are used. It is possible to staple the reeds on by hand with fencing staples, but I prefer to use an 18 gauge staple gun attached to my compressor. The 22mm gal staples go into timber easily and hold the reed mats firmly. Considering I have used 10,000 staples on a house I worked on, I think it would have been a long process putting them in by hand. Some days I have used over 1000 staples!

On smaller expanses of timber or steel, gutter guard has proved to be quick and easy. Sold in rolls the plastic mesh is just like plasterboard tape on a larger scale.

When using gutter guard to cover 45mm stud work we usually cut the roll in half with a fine toothed hand saw first. For steel or timber framing to 100mm wide it works great straight off the roll. Whenever possible I staple the gutter guard onto timber, otherwise the wire pins are used to attach the mesh to the bales. The same wire pins are used to pin the reed mats to the bales. Once the render has encased the mesh and set, the pinning is irrelevant. We only need to hold it there until the render is applied.

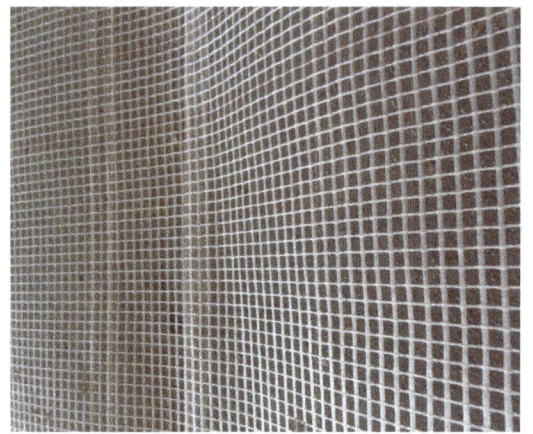

Acrylic render mesh is used similarly to gutter guard and is sold in large rolls. It is really handy to have around as it can be cut to any size or shape. It needs to be put on top of a recently applied render and trowled in because the holes in the mesh are too small to allow render to properly go through. This can lead to poor bonding with the substrate and delamination. Some builders cover the entire wall with the acrylic render mesh as part of a three coat sand clay rendering system. Most often these builders use rendering pumps and do not use straw clay render at all. Generally the mesh is trowled into the second coat until it is not visible.

The three coat sand clay system that uses the acrylic render mesh is a proven consistent performer. I find in my own work that by making the walls as solid as possible before rendering, I can get away with only meshing the timber, steel and reveals. This is probably due to the straw clay render being so full of fibre and inherent meshing strength. If any cracks do appear in the straw clay render once it has dried I dig them out a little and cover them with mesh and a little more render. This is allowed to dry before the sand clay coat goes over the top. Any structural crack in the straw clay render that is not fixed in this manner will go right through the sand clay render top coat and be far more difficult to repair.

Nails are used to provide extra grip on large expanses of timer or on the sides of posts. The straw clay render grips onto the nails and will maintain a bond even when the post shrinks over time. All the window and door reveals on the houses I build are detailed in such a way that straw clay render is used to create the shape desired. Many nails are nailed into the framing to hold the straw clay render in place. Once dry sand clay render is used as a top coat. Galvanised nails or screws are the best to use as they don't rust over time. It is the straw in the clay render that maintains a strong fibrous matrix in the render.

On many mud brick house repair jobs I have had to dig out old mud mortar around doors and posts that had cracked and crumbled away. Most of the time the mortar used did not contain any straw. This mortar was often used to fill in between the bricks and posts without any nails or mesh on the posts. Years later I am called in to dig out what is left, put in lots of screws or nails into the posts and fill the space back up with straw clay render. This render is compressed very well a few times whilst drying.

Sometimes the hole in the wall is way too big for mesh or reeds to cover. Most often this is found on straw bale houses above the windows and doors. Occasionally a straw bale house is designed so that the windows and doors fit in between the bale courses. As this is a very limiting detail most straw bale houses designers just let the builders sort out the weird sized void. Over the years I have seen and used many different

methods of filling these spots with varied success. Now I have started to use wattle and daub as my preferred method. The straw clay render is used as the daub and timber used as the wattle. Any shape can be easily created with timber and the whole lot gets 100mm of straw clay render. The timber laths used as the wattle end up becoming embedded in the middle of the render, 50mm each side. This creates a super strong matrix of straw, clay and timber. The main things to remember is setting the wattles 50mm back from the wall surface you are trying to create. Then once dry the wattle and daub section gets rendered with the rest of the wall. I like to mesh the area where the wattles end to help minimise cracking in this area.

## Mixing straw clay on a tarpaulin

The Cob revival, led by Ianto Evens of Cob Cottage Company fame, developed and spread widely the technique of mixing cob on a tarp. It is a basic and surprisingly effective method of mixing material manually. Hundreds of cob cottages have been built using this method. My cob cottage was.

Tarp mixing is also a fantastic way to mix straw clay render. Taking off ones shoes and socks

before jumping into a pile of wet mud is often a person's first exposure to earth building. Such a confronting and intimate bonding with the earth can cause hesitation and resistance from some people. Once that first step is taken a whole new world opens up as we throw off some of the shackles of modern day norms and start playing with the clay mother. I have mixed cob, light earth, earth floor mix, pizza oven mud and straw clay render with my bare feet. I prefer the blue 5 by 8 feet tarps as they are cheap and have the size to move the material around properly.

To mix a batch of straw clay render on a tarp find a flattish area with no stones or rocks lying around. Lay out the tarp, add the sand and spread it out a little. Then, add the clay on top of the sand. The sand is added first in an attempt to stop the clay sticking so much to the tarp after a few mixes have been made on it.

Walk to one end of the tarp and pick up the two corners along the short side of the tarp. Holding the corners together walk to the other end as far as you can, turning the mix until it almost falls off the tarp. Then, picking up the corners at the other end, walk the mix back to the centre of the tarp. It is important to note here that earth is very heavy! Whenever you are mixing or moving earth on a tarp keep a straight back and always ask for help.

Earth building should be a joyous occasion not a body destroying activity. The clay and sand should be mixed a little after the run backwards and forwards on the tarp. Make a doughnut or well in the centre and pour in half a bucket of water. With your bare feet mix the water into the clay and sand a little. Use the tarp to turn the mix over and your feet to stomp the mix together. Add water as you go until the mix is uniform and contains enough moisture to receive the straw.

The straw will dry the mix up quite a bit, but it is easier to add more water than take it away so don't add too much!

Add the straw and start mixing the whole lot together with your feet. At this point it is easiest to go back to the original method of grabbing the two short corners together and walking to the other end. A big roll of render will be formed with the dry straw in the middle.

Starting at one end of the roll stomp the roll flat all the way to the other end. When flat, roll it up again and flatten it again. After a few times of flattening and rolling the mix should be ready.

Grab a friend and drag, not carry the render to the wall that is being rendered. Alternatively, fork it into a wheelbarrow and wheel it to the wall.

For small jobs or group projects, mixing on tarps is the way to go. There is no noise or dangerous machines involved. The whole process is therapeutic. A little music, live or otherwise can really help to create an enjoyable scene.

## Mixing render with a Larry hoe in a wheelbarrow:

One of the cheapest and useful mixing tools available is the Larry hoe - also known as a mortar mixing hoe. The Larry looks like a garden hoe that has had two large round holes cut out of it. These holes create the swirls and currents in the mortar as its being mixed. The holes are what makes the Larry so efficient at what is does.

I use my Larry to mix concrete, brick mortar, lime mortar, lime render, sand clay render and the base of straw clay render. Once the base of the straw clay render is mixed the hands are used to mix the straw in to finish off the mix.

Place a little water in your wheelbarrow or tub and add the clay. It can help to let the clay sit for a minute to allow the capillary action of the water to soften the clay.

Starting at one end of the wheelbarrow, run the Larry down the barrows base. Flick it towards yourself. Flick is the appropriate word here as we want lots of little low weight movements rather than few heavy ones. In this way we don't get tired or hurt. Keep running the Larry down the front of the barrow, flicking the mix towards you. You want to try to get all the material off the base of the barrow to ensure there are no dry spots.

Next, head to the other end of the barrow and repeat, adding water as needed. The Larry should be riding on the plastic or metal base of the barrow at all times.

When the mix looks done and the water content right, start running the Larry backward and forwards just below the surface. This will bring the holes into play and help to thoroughly mix the materials. I like to go forwards and backwards 4 or 5 times near the surface and then mix deeper to bring up some material from the bottom.

Short straw can be added if it is required. Or long straw can be added and mixed in with your hands. Keep mixing until the render is the consistency you want. It is hard to find a more useful tool than the larry hoe.

## Mixing clay render in a concrete mixer:

The concrete mixer is found on most construction sites. It is often the first piece of large equipment that new comers are exposed to. Predominately used for mixing mortar for brick laying, concrete mixers can also be used to mix concrete, clay slip and sand clay renders.

Some people claim you can mix cob in a concrete mixer. I think it is way too slow and the soupy mess resembles render more than it resembles cob.

Personally I like to use machines for what they were designed for, as it puts less stress on the machine. Being a machine, the concrete mixer should be treated with respect. Don't put your shovel in that barrel if you like your shoulders in their sockets. Never turn the machine on under load, and, if there is a mix in the barrel, keep it moving.

The best way to learn how to mix in a concrete mixer is to work as a brickies labourer for a while. If that is not possible the following pointers may help.

To start a mix, turn the machine on and pour in or spray some water all over the barrel. Next, add some of the sand that is needed for the render mix you are doing. The sand will help to clean the inside of the barrel from the previous mix and hopefully stop the clay from sticking to the inside of the mixer. Add more water until all of the sand is wet and moving freely. You do not want any material stuck to the barrel at this stage.

Add all of the clay that is going into the mix with enough water so that the clay blends into the sand and is moving freely.

Finally, add the remaining sand to dry the mix out to the consistency you desire. You may need to add more water.

Look carefully at how the mix is falling off the tines inside the barrel. This is a major indication of the moisture content of the mix. Learn to recognise how the mix looks when it is just what you want.

Position your wheelbarrow in a good spot to empty the mixer. Be very careful unloading as a full mixer is heavy. Empty the mix into your wheelbarrow and spray or pour some water into the still moving barrel to clean it. Adding a shovel of sand at this stage will really help to keep the barrel clean - just remember to add one less shovel of sand when doing your next mix.

I was taught to add material to the mixer, aggregate first, then binder.

For a lime render it was 3 shovels of sand, then one shovel of lime. This was repeated 4 times per mix. Now, as previously described, I prefer to add a little of the sand to clean the barrel, then add all of the clay or lime to get it thoroughly mixed. Finally I add the rest of the sand to dry the mix down to a useable state. This change in procedure occurred while I was working predominately with clay renders. The clay component is often very sticky. I also find lime to be quite sticky. So now I mix all my mixes in this way and have better results.

At the end of the day be sure to clean out the mixer really well. A high quality concrete mixer is an asset on a building site, one that should be respected and looked after.

## Mixing straw clay render with a rotary hoe:

A rotary hoe or rota tiller can become an earth builders best friend. With a small investment in money and a little time to learn the skills, huge quantities of cob or render can be produced.

The rotary hoe brings speed, efficiency and affordability to the heavier unruly earth mixes. It is no longer such a slow process mixing cob or straw clay render. That is not to say that I don't mix cob and straw clay render with my bare feet every once in a while and love it! By using the rotary hoe I can justify using those materials much more on jobs as they become cost effective by using the machine to help do the work.

The machine you need is a front tine rotary hoe of a decent enough size to handle the heavy work. Small front tine machines don't really have enough power to handle the load. Rear tine machines do not really do what we want and may cut your toes off!

The Massport model I own is absolutely perfect at mixing cob and straw clay render. The long front end coupled with small tines that don't bend too much makes one think that it was designed for this sort of work. That said I have owned others in the past that have mixed up tons of cob with no problem. The only real problem is trying to buy a half decent front tine rotary hoe. I was lucky to get mine from an online auction.

To mix straw clay render it is easiest to chop the straw up a little with your mulcher or whipper snipper first. This will make the render easier to mix and apply. If the straw is too long it can tangle around the tines too much, especially if your rotary hoe has L-shaped tines. That said, I have mixed lots of straw clay render with straw straight off the bale.

Aussie straw normally comes from short stemmed varieties and the droughts we have been having is making it even shorter. I will assume that the straw you will be using is chopped up into lengths 100mm and less. The bulk of the straw is best between 25 and 50mm. The mix you use will have to be tested before mixing big batches. I will assume you will use a mix of 2 parts sub-soil to one part chopped straw.

To start find a nice flattish place to mix. Road bases are good. Concrete, asphalt and grass is not so good.

The mixing process will probably draw up some of the base you are working on while mixing, so make sure its compatible with your mix.

Measure out eight to ten buckets of sub-soil and spread them out to approximately 100mm deep in a well shape - just like making dough with the sides a little higher to contain water.

Spray or bucket in a fair amount of water and let it soak in a bit. Start your rotary hoe and start making runs through the pile swerving from side to side. You want to just be touching the road base with the tines. Pulling the machine backwards through the mix is also effective. Most likely you will have to stop, add some water and reassemble the pile into a workable form. Add the straw at this point and keep mixing and turning the pile over until it is like what you want.

The amount of moisture in the mix is very important and hard to gauge. Peoples opinion about the moisture content of straw clay render varies widely. It is really all about balancing the dual characteristics of ease of application and low slump. If a mix it is too dry it is hard to apply and your body will tire out quickly. Too wet a mix and it

will end up on the floor, slumping and will very likely crack as well. You will have to rely on your own personal experience here.

Once the pile of clay and straw resembles render, mound it all up into a pile. At this stage I like to stomp around in the mix with my gumboots to give it a final once over and check the moisture content.

Then I pile the mix up again before forking it into a wheelbarrow for delivery. I prefer half full wheelbarrows as this is one heavy brew. If it is a hot day cover the pile straight away with a tarp to stop water loss. Repeat as needed.

To mix cob it is the same process, but use clay mixed with a well graded sand and less straw.

## Mixing clay paint with a paint mixing drill

Clay paint, clay slip and sand clay render can all be mixed with a paint mixing drill. A paint mixing drill usually has two large handles, adjustable speed and a permanently attached mixing paddle.

On job sites you will see plasterers mix base coat mud and tilers mix tile adhesive with paint mixing drills. The drill is large enough to handle the strain of mixing the heavier mixes. I usually only use my paint mixing drill, or egg beater as it has come to be known, for mixing clay paint, clay slip and sand clay render. I have used the paint mixing drill to mix straw clay render a few times. It definitely puts too much strain on the poor thing.

On larger jobs I find I need a larger volume of material when I'm mixing sand clay render than can be mixed quickly with the paint mixing drill. A concrete mixer is far better suited to the bigger jobs.

A 30 litre bucket is the best to mix in as it has high sides to help contain what you are mixing. Usually, on jobs, all the materials are prepared before rendering work begins, a few batches being made at a time.

If using pigment in the paint the amount of material and pigment must be very accurately followed. A digital scale is best for measuring pigment to ensure consistency. A cook stove will be needed if the paint contains wheat paste.

It is best to get everything set up like a big kitchen. A drop sheet or tarp is good to have on the floor to contain spills. Firstly, the pigment must be thoroughly mixed with the water. I tend to start by using half of the water I think will be needed when making the first batch. During the mixing of the first batch more water will need to be added here and there to achieve the desired thickness. Then, I record the total volume of water I used in making the first batch and use this amount in all the other batches.

Mix the pigment for quite a while and have a good look to see if any bits have not mixed in properly. Once your happy the pigment is well mixed it is time to add the glue.

Make sure the casein or wheat paste glue is strained through a kitchen strainer as it is being poured into the bucket. Mix again for a minute and check the thickness.

If all is mixed well it is time to start adding the dry ingredients. The amount of clay, sand and talc used in the paint having already been worked out and tested, I like to add the clay first while the mixture is still full of liquid. I think this helps to mix the clay into the paint more thoroughly. Mix well and add the sand or talc and mix again.

At this stage the paint may appear to be a little thinner than desired. This is due to the fact that we have not added the glue which will thicken up the mix for us.

Make sure the casein or wheat paste glue is strained through a kitchen strainer as it is being poured into the bucket.

Mix again for a minute and check the thickness.

Pour the paint through a fine kitchen sieve into a clean bucket.

Note the exact amount of water used if it was the first batch and get painting.

# Part 3 Tools for the Earth builder

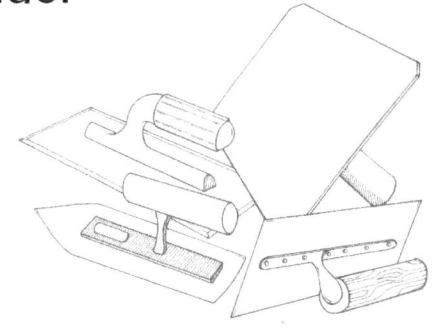

The tools listed in this section of the book are a selection of the tools used regularly by professional earth builders in their day-to-day work. You can build an earthen home with nothing but a strong body and a tarp. Many cob buildings have been built this way. For those of us that work daily as professional earth builders we need to work quickly and efficiently. Body efficiency is critical to the professional earth builder if they desire a long term career as wet earth is heavy and the human body is relatively weak. The tools covered in this section are specific earth building tools that are reached for again and again during our work.

Obviously other basic tools are needed on-site for daily operations, such as an air compressor to run the staple gun and a wheelbarrow to move mud around in. Ladders, planks and scaffold also come to mind but are not covered here in detail.

Clay is different to other binders in that it can be easily cleaned off tools after it has dried. This fact can allow one to become slack at cleaning the tools at the end of each day. Personally I enjoy the ritual of cleaning all the tools at the end of the day. It is the ritual of the tradesperson. Metal tools will rust instantly if clay is allowed to dry on them. Non stainless steel trowels get destroyed in this way as the rust pits the surface of the trowel making it rough. It is a good idea to keep all trowels clean when not in use, wash them in clean water and dry them with a cloth. A good tradesperson honours their tools and treats them with love.

As earth building is hard and heavy work, high quality tools are recommended. I think it is better to have a few good quality tools, than lots of low quality ones. Some of the tools on this list can be made or will have to be made. Others can be found in back sheds, at garage sales and markets or on the numerous internet trading sites. It is generally cheaper to buy tools this way and you should get higher quality tools than what is available these days at your local hardware. Over the years the quality of tools has declined to a point where one has to search out real quality. I like the feel of history in the old tools. It is as if you soak up some of their previous owners experience. The main things to buy new and to properly look after are your two main trowels, the hard and the flexible trowel. Try as many different types of trowels as you can before buying. Different trowels suit different people. The shape and size of the handle can feel very different to different people depending on your hand size.

## Hands

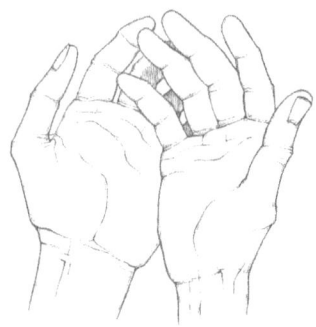

The most basic, useful and often used tools on any job site are one's hands. It is important to keep yours in good condition by wearing gloves when working with lime or cement. It is not necessary to use gloves when working with clay as it is non-toxic and actually has a healing quality to it. The clay will dry your hands out as it draws toxins from the body, so a good quality hand cream is welcomed at the end of each day.

Hands can be used for mixing renders, for applying render and even for smoothing it out. People have been doing so ever since they started building with clay. Tools came later to help people achieve different finishes and to improve speed. Don't underestimate the power of your hands to form an intimate bond with the clay itself.

## Sponges

Sponges have been used to smooth out renders for a long time. Sea sponges and luffas were widely used before the more modern synthetic ones were available. Sponges are also used to clean up around the working area, to wipe off timbers and even to clean tools.

There is a large variation in sponges - from the ones to clean your dishes with, to fine rendering sponges. The ones to look for have very few holes in them, as the holes pick up sand and make a rough surface. A tight sponge will make a smooth wall. When to sponge and how wet the sponge should be is something that one learns with experience. Generally, if the sponge is making the surface rougher, then it is too soon to use a sponge.

## Paint Brushes

Paint brushes have multiple uses around the job site. I use them dry as little brooms to brush clay and sand grains away from work areas - especially useful in tight corners. A dampened paint brush is useful to smooth out areas of render that are hard to sponge. This comes in handy when doing relief work or rendering niches. A little bit of render can be brushed onto trouble spots with the brush and then the brush is cleaned, moistened and the spot smoothed out with the same brush. Wet paint brushes are useful in cleaning up the edges where render touches wood. Larger brushes are good for painting walls. Specialty lime wash brushes work great for clay paints. I mainly use the cheap natural bristled disposable brushes as they don't have too many bristles. The big problem with clay paints is the grit. A paint brush with lots of bristles gets clogged easily and is then hard to clean. The cheaper brushes with less bristles clog less and clean more easily.

## Dustpan Brush

The dustpan brush is used just like the paint brush. They come in handy to clean up around the site and to paint large areas with clay paint. Many mud brick houses in Australia have been painted with dust pan brushes over the years. The short bristles and comfortable handle make them idea for the job. I have come to use the dust pan brushes for final finishing on renders. If the wall is brushed at the right time any excess sand is swept away and the render compressed. This step can make a huge difference to the finished result. The render has to be dry enough so that the bristles do not leave any brush marks, but still damp enough to be compressed. The wooden handled, natural fibre dustpan brushes work the best for this.

## Wood Float

Wood floats are used extensively in earth building. Being a wooden trowel, the float is used as a trowel and as a compression device. The wood will not stick to the clay if it is kept clean and damp. Because it's wood the surface of the render or floor will not

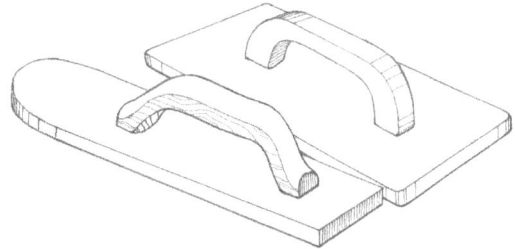

get sealed off and so can dry out properly. Also, the wood will not draw the water to the surface like a steel trowel will. This means that all the clay binder stays distributed throughout the mix. This is important for creating the strongest possible renders and floors.

When applying straw-clay render the wood float is used to shape the wall, just after your hand has applied the render. As the render starts to dry the same float is used to compress and further shape the straw-clay. The process is the same when installing earth floors. During compression new material can be added to fill in holes or defects, the new material is compressed in with the wood float and almost unrecognisable upon drying. Often a steel trowel is used after compression to get the nice smooth surface.

When buying a wooden float there a few things to consider. Firstly not all woods work that great for earth building. I have tried 10 different woods and find that Sweitenia Mahogany works the best. This is a plantation grown timber from south America that is grown in SE Asia. It is possible to buy mahogany wood floats on the internet from the

USA. I buy slabs of Sweitenia Mahogany from a furniture timber shop and make my own floats. The problem is that they wear out. Other Australian timber may work, try and see. Once you have used a mahogany one you will understand what I mean.

## Poly Float

Poly floats are used in the place of wood floats for compressing sand clay renders. As sand clay renders are thinner than straw clay render they seem to go off quicker. A wood float can often leave stains on a light coloured sand clay render if it has started to go off, where a poly float won't.

As the sand clay renders are generally flatter you do not need to do as much grinding, so the need to use wood to stop the binder being pulled to the surface does not seem as important. The poly floats come in a few different sizes. Generally the larger the float, the flatter the wall will become.

## Hawk

The hawk is a flat piece of wood or metal with some type of handle used to hold render while applying it. They come in American / European types and Japanese types. The most common is the American / European type. I have come to prefer the Japanese type over the years as you can put them down

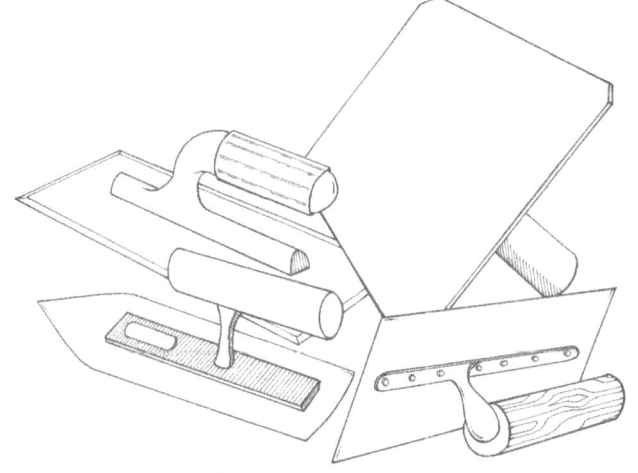

when they have render on them - they are also more comfortable to use. It is quite easy to make a Japanese style hawk out of plywood and scrap timber. Most Japanese earth builders make their own.

## Hard trowel

The hard trowel is the basic render-applying work horse on a job site. Everyone has their own favourite shape and size. The hardness of the steel makes the application more difficult as the wall has to be quite flat to be smoothed out. This is a good thing as it teaches us good rendering technique and makes the following compression and polishing easier. This does not mean that all your walls have to be flat, it is just that the planes have to be consistent. If you apply render with a flexible trowel it is hard to get a good final result. These trowels are either sold as Finishing Trowels or as Concrete Trowels.

## Flexible Trowel

The flexible trowels I use are all made in Japan specifically for earth rendering. They come in a variety of sizes and shapes. Generally they are made of thin stainless steel with a small wooden handle. The flexibility allows us to get a perfectly smooth wall after compression, even if the wall is not 100% flat. They come in handy for doing repairs on existing render, as it is easy to fan out the edges with the flexible trowel. I also use them when earth rendering over plasterboard, as they are light and easy to work with. It is also possible to get Italian polishing trowels. They are really nice and don't wear out like the Japanese ones, but you need to use them on a really flat wall.

## Plastic Trowel

Plastic trowels are used to polish clay renders. If polishing is left for too long a stainless steel trowel will leave oxidation stains on the render. In this case a plastic trowel is needed as it does not leave the oxidation stains. You can easily obtain the red plastic trowels from most places as people use them when applying acrylic render. Other plastic trowels are also available. In different thicknesses and shapes.

## Inside Corner Trowel

Inside corner trowels are freely available in the plasterboard section of your hardware store. Mainly used to stop up interior plasterboard corners, they also come in handy when rendering. It depends on the finished look of the building that the clients want. The side walls have to be quite flat to use an interior trowel properly. There are some smaller ones out there that are a little more forgiving.

## Outside Corner Trowel

Outside corner trowels are also available at most hardware stores. They are used more in acrylic render and plasterboard jobs than with earth 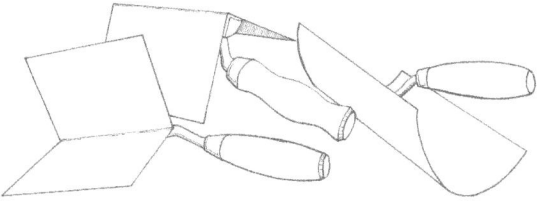 building. It is not that you cannot use them more widely, it is just that the external corners of earth buildings are usually rounded. This is because earth render is not super strong and really sharp exterior corners are easily damaged. Still, they do come in handy to rough in the lines of the exterior corners, then a sponge or trowel is used later to round the corner off. In this way a super clean exterior corner can be created.

## Curved Inside Corner Trowel

Curved interior trowels do exist in Japan and probably a few other countries. I have managed to pick up an old trowel made for doing curb and channel that works great. Previously I just made my own inside corner trowels out of plastic pipe with a handle screwed onto it. It is best to sand the edges a little so that they don't grab. Ideally you need two trowels, one slightly larger than the other. The larger one is used with the straw-clay render to rough in the shape. The smaller one is used with the sand clay render to get a smooth finish.

## Putty Knife / Small Tool

Putty knives and small tools come in handy to get to those small difficult spots. They are also used to scrape splashed render off timber and plasterboard. Many people have a favourite putty knife or small tool that they use when working on the more artistic elements of earthen render, such as relief and niches. It is often a good idea to re-compress the edges of the render where it meets wood or plasterboard the next morning after application. This helps to strengthen those areas and clean up such critical details.

## Bread Knife

A serrated bread knife has lots of uses on an earth building job site. Often mud bricks, light earth or render has to be trimmed back. As these all have straw in them the serrations are needed to cut through the straw. Without the serrations the clay just crumbles and falls away leaving the straw behind to get in the way. I find the bread knife handy to open up the gap between old mud bricks and posts in preparation for repairing.

## Fencing Pliers

Earth and straw buildings need lots of metal pins made from fencing wire when attaching mesh and reeds to them. The good old farmers fencing pliers are built for the job. There is a slot at the top of them that the wire is slid through and bent backwards to make the pins. The hammer head is then used to bash the pins into the wall. The sharp point at the other end comes in handy to scratch up walls prior to rendering. You can easily pick up an old pair from your local market for a few bucks. Fencing pliers also come in handy when bailing houses as often straw bale buildings will also be compressed with fencing wire.

## Bale Needle

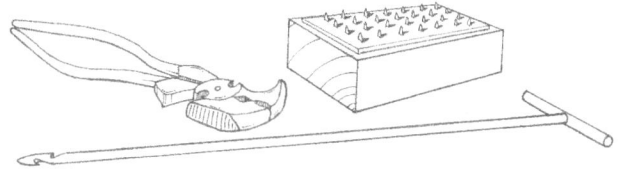

Bale needles come in many shapes and sizes. Mainly used to re-size straw bales during wall filling, bale needles also come in handy when stitching walls, either for external pinning or mesh work. I often use the bale needle to poke baling twine through a light earth wall to help pull hoop iron bracing closer in pre-render. Once a electrician used it to get a wire through a light earth wall. A key slot is preferable to a hole at the end of the needle as it is easier to get the twine in.

## Bum Scrubber

A bum scrubber is a homemade, oversized rasp. This is used mainly to flatten the string ends of straw bales before stacking them into the wall. In this way most of the voids in between the straw bales in straw bale walls are eliminated. Not only do you get a better insulated wall, but you don't have to run around packing stuff in all the holes pre-render. A gang nail plate is used to make the bum scrubber. All of the nail bits are nailed out and the plate is attached to a piece of 70mm by 35mm timber with staples. It is handy to spray paint the bum scrubber a bright colour so you don't loose it. The bum scrubber also doubles as a handy scratcher if you have an old wall that need scratching up before rendering.

## Mud Brick Moulds

Mud brick moulds are needed to make mud bricks. I have five or six different sizes of moulds for different applications. The standard one for making bricks I mainly use in restoration work. I have a house brick size

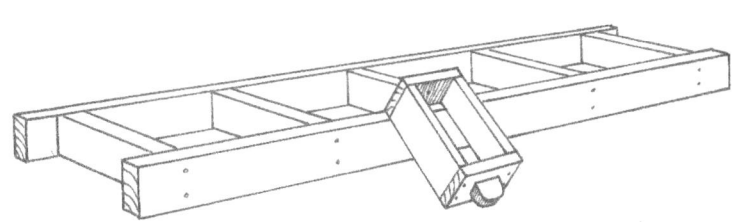

one for building small stuff. I have one the size used for vaults and domes, just in case my future takes me there. I also have one 405mm long by 90mm wide to make bricks to put in between studs internally to make mass walls. All of these moulds have been made with scrap timber and a few screws - with some handles on the side. I prefer the single moulds as they are easier to clean than gang moulds.

## Tubs

Plasterer's tubs are made from either plastic or rubber. Most are rectangular inside and hold about half a wheelbarrow load of material. The uses of tubs are wide ranging on and off job sites. When testing render mixes or on smaller jobs, render can be mixed in the tub itself. Then the tub can be carried to the wall. Tubs 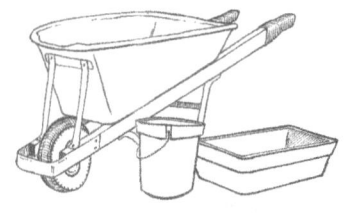 are used to hold bulk render, cob and light earth when working off planks or scaffold. During clean up the tubs come in handy to get all of the floor sweepings and leftovers out of the building. Small quantities of sand can be screened into tubs. When packing the ute for a job big or small, the tubs are one of the first thing loaded and no matter how many I take there is never enough.

## Larry

The Larry is a mortar mixing hoe. It is based on a standard garden hoe but has two quite large round holes cut out of it. When mixing wet mortar or render the material swirls through these holes, making mixing quicker and easier. It is always a good idea to have a Larry in a wheelbarrow of render. Then anyone can quickly and easily remix the render prior to application. If you cannot afford a concrete mixer a Larry will quickly become your best friend.

## Fork

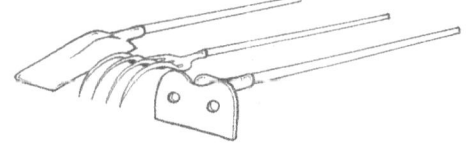

Garden forks are handy on job sites to move around material. Cob, light earth and straw clay render are all far more easily moved with a fork than a shovel. Look for a fork with close together tines so that the material does not fall through too much. A long handle can be nice when moving material up onto scaffold or planks.`

## Texture Gun

The texture gun is a small hopper type spray unit that attaches to a standard air compressor designed to spray plasterboard mud onto walls and ceilings to create decorative effects. Often used in the USA but seldom seen in Australia, the texture gun is a huge asset to straw bale builders. They are available in Australia for around $100. The texture gun will spray clay slip

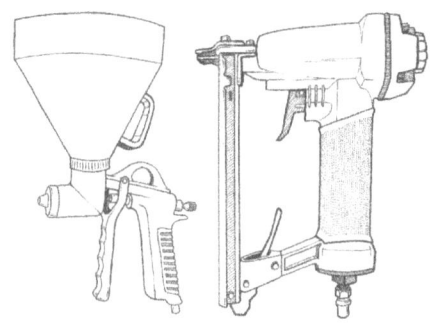

deep into straw bales with ease. The clay slip is made first with a drill or concrete mixer. Then the texture gun is filled a few litres at a time and the wall is sprayed. I often also spray clay slip onto light earth walls before rendering them with the straw clay render. It is best to just spray the section of the wall you are working on, so that the clay slip does not dry out before the render is applied.

## 18 Gauge Stapler

The 18 gauge stapler is a nail gun designed for staples. It runs off a standard air compressor. The staples are used to attach mesh and reeds to timber. Pre-render we will use 3000 to 5000 staples to attach all the mesh and reeds over the timber sections of the house to be rendered. The staplers can be bought for $60 at some hardware stores, but they only last a job or two due to metal fatigue. I have had much more success buying higher priced models.

The staples come in a few different sizes, I like to use 25mm galvanised ones for all applications.

## Paint Mixing Drill

The large paint mixing drill, or 'the egg beater' as mine got named normally has two big handles and a fixed paddle. Designed to mix paint, plasterboard mud and tile adhesive. They also do a

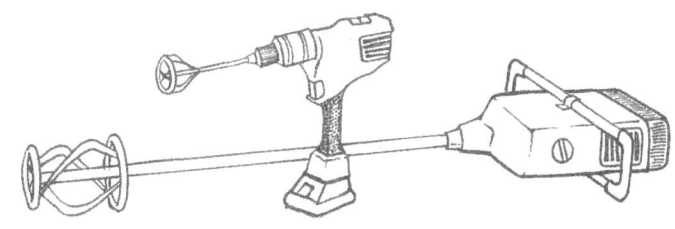

great job of mixing sand-clay render, clay paint and clay slip. I have mixed straw clay render with mine once or twice, but it did not like it too much. The most important thing to remember with the drill is to thoroughly clean the mixer after each batch. If you forget you will inevitably get some hard lumps of stuff you don't want in a future batch.

## Concrete Mixer

Buy a good one and it will not let you down. I have had too many issues with cheap ones and seen lots of jobs stall due to them. They are often dangerous too. A concrete mixer is run flat out all day on some sites, filled with heavy wet mud. Do not underestimate the dangers of concrete mixers used for mixing clay slip and sand clay render. Lime render, brick mortar and concrete can be mixed in these also. Generally, for earth building, the more tines in the mixer, the better.

## Rotary Hoe

A front tine rotary hoe can mix large quantities of straw clay render or cob easily. Well it is still hard work but it is fast. Don't even bother with a rear tine model. Different models perform differently, but they all work. You just have to spend a little time experimenting with mixing before you get it worked out. The critical thing to work out is moisture content and what you don't have to do - like do I need to screen that sub-soil? Do I need to chop that straw? Probably 'yes' to the straw question as it catches around the tines otherwise.

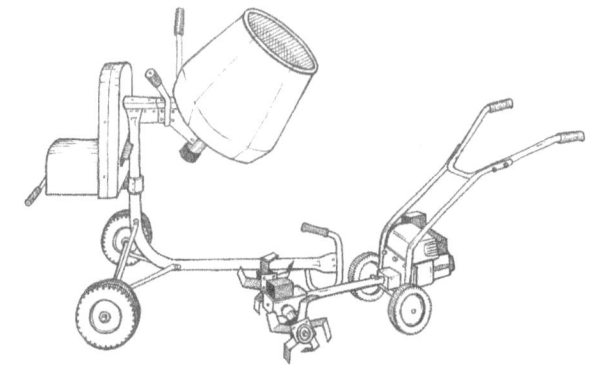

## Whipper Snipper

Whipper snippers are used to chop up straw. A plastic 200 litre barrel is filled 1/3 of the way up with straw and a brave person with eye protection and a dust mask chops it up with the whipper snipper. Dusty, noisy and not too much fun, but super effective and, everyone seems to have a whipper snipper.

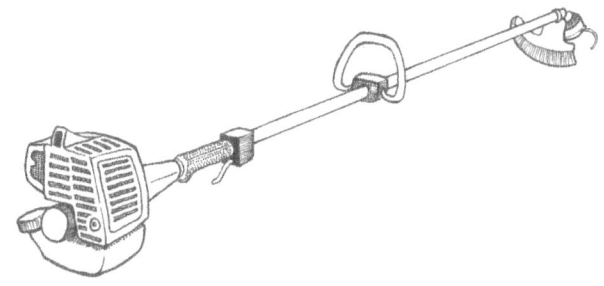

The straw is chopped up a little for rotary hoe cob mixes and chopped up a little more for straw clay render. It is possible to chop it up really fine before screening the straw through a 6mm screen if you want to use it in sand clay renders.

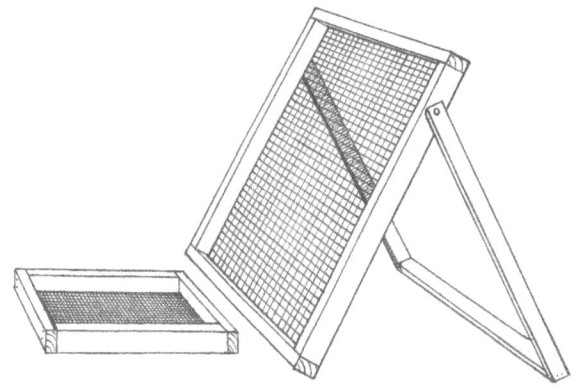

## Shopping List of Tools for the Earth Builder:
© James Henderson 2013

- ☐ Sponge
- ☐ Paint Brushes
- ☐ Dustpan Brush
- ☐ Wood Float
- ☐ Poly Float
- ☐ Hawk
- ☐ Hard trowel
- ☐ Flexible Trowel
- ☐ Plastic Trowel
- ☐ Inside Corner Trowel
- ☐ Outside Corner Trowel
- ☐ Curved Inside Corner Trowel
- ☐ Putty Knife
- ☐ Bread Knife
- ☐ Fencing Pliers
- ☐ Mud Brick Moulds
- ☐ Bale Needle
- ☐ Bum Scrubber
- ☐ Tubs
- ☐ Larry
- ☐ Fork
- ☐ Texture Gun
- ☐ 18 Gauge Stapler
- ☐ Paint Mixing Drill
- ☐ Concrete Mixer
- ☐ Rotary Hoe
- ☐ Whipper Snipper

From Earth Render The art of clay plaster, render and paints by James Henderson
Published by Python Press    ISBN 978-0-9757782-0-3
Illustrations by Mike Angliss

# References

1. Allen, C. 1854
Rudimentary Treatise on Cottage Building, or, Hints For Improving the Dwellings of the Labouring Classes
London, England
Hughes Printer

2. Kong, A. 1984
An Experimental Study on the effects of straw on drying and shrinkage of Mud Bricks
Published in "The Proceedings Owner – Building and Earth Architecture. National Conference 3 – 5 Feb. 1984. Melbourne   Australia
University of Melbourne Press

3. Bainbridge, D.; Steen, B and A.; Eisenberg, D. 1994
The Straw Bale House
White River Junction, Vermont, USA
Chelsea Green Publishing.

4. Edwards, R. Wei – Hao, L. 1984
Mud Brick and Earth Building the Chinese Way
Kuranda, Qld, Australia
The Rams Skull Press

5. Reynolds, Emily
Japan's Clay Walls
A Glimpse into their Tradition of Plastering
Peace Street Publications

6. Minke, Gernot
Building With Earth
Birkhäuser, 2009
Basel, Switzerland

## PYTHON PRESS

Books on sensitive and sustainable living, esoteric agriculture and awareness of the spiritual dimensions of life and planet.
Available at bookstores around the world or buy directly from:
**www.pythonpress.com**
eMail: pythonpress@gmail.com

# The Sheltermaker's Manual
## Volume 1
### by Peter Cowman
architect, eco-builder, writer, international teacher & director of the Living Architecture Centre

294 page paperback, 189X246mm
ISBN: 978-0-9757782-6-5

PYTHON PRESS

In this innovative and supremely practical Manual Peter Cowman articulates what can only be described as the secrets of vernacular architecture or as he calls it 'sheltermaking'.

With its emphasis on the positive the practical and the affordable The Sheltermaker's Manual articulates a proven design methodology for the creation of versatile and meaningful designs suited to the modern world, information which can be applied both to new as well as to existing buildings - in whatever part of the world one happens to live.

The Sheltermaker's Manual also offers people the opportunity to understand the hidden psychological aspects of 'home'. Such 'intangibles' are utilised as a means of exploring ones' inner self in an effort to uncover 'the dream house within'. On this level, the Manual operates as a self-development tool, allowing people to resolve personal life issues, oftentimes without the need, or expense, of building at all! So, you don't have to want to build in order to justify buying this book. You need it to inform yourself and to understand how our houses can assist us in achieving a sustainable way-of-life.

The Manual's Design Programme clearly sets out a unique and proven design methodology - when the process of planning, investigating, costing and decision-making has been completed, only then is the plan of the building put together. This is in contrast to normal design practice where the plan is the first thing that is created which can lead to insurmountable problems, as can be witnessed in many professionally designed homes. The Design Programme structure also facilitates the importation of outside information into the design equation.

The Sheltermaker's Manual has evolved from the unique Be Your Own Architect Courses which Peter Cowman first presented in 1989. Written in an accessible and practical style and featuring over 900 illustrations, the Manual reveals information not previously available on the subject of house design.

Details of completed projects are included in the Manual, plus information on the EconoSpace, a unique low-cost eco-building featuring the original peter-post framing system.

## What Sheltermakers have to say about their use of the Manual ...
'To give over control of your house design to someone else is asking for trouble'
'Living space is just that - it's part of who you are and how you feel'
'I can't imagine building a house and allowing someone else to tell you your needs and wants!'
'I believe that there is not another way'

# The Sheltermaker's Manual
## Volume 2
### by Peter Cowman
architect, eco-builder, writer, international teacher & director of the Living Architecture Centre

347 page paperback, 189X246mm

ISBN: 978-0-9757782-7-2

PYTHON PRESS

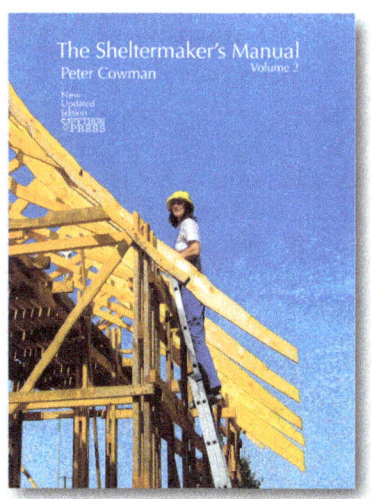

There are many hidden aspects to the process of 'sheltermaking'. Peter Cowman refers to these as the 'invisible architecture'. Unseen yet powerful in their effect, one will ignore these at one's peril!

We are invited to think of this invisible architecture not just in terms of physical buildings but also in terms of our dream world and the lives we have to live. When we become aware of the power of this 'living of one's architecture' we are presented with a dynamic tool for practical change in our lives.

In this indispensable companion to Volume 1, revelation of the mysteries of sheltermaking can be said to be complete. With its roots in Sacred Geometry, Feng Shui and Vastu Shastra traditions this Manual will forever change how we think of architecture, houses and even ourselves!

Building on the firm foundation laid down in Volume 1 this volume deals with the selection of appropriate materials and their assembly. Also covered are plumbing, drainage and electrical services, planning and site selection, and, the all important layout when the plan is assembled. Costing and the preparation of planning and working drawings are covered also.

'What Sheltermakers have to say about their use of the Manual ...
'It's wonderful to have a home specially designed to meet your needs and lifestyle'
'I feel I would be fit to face almost any challenge in the future'
'I loved the design process and found that I was good at it!'
'Made me more aware of the space I am in'
'I feel that quality of my life has increased'
'I realised nobody else can live our life'
'I love my home and coming home'
'A very empowering experience'
'Shook up lots of assumptions'
'A great sense of achievement'
'Lots of feelgood factor'
'The right thing to do'
'A bit like giving birth'
'Very fulfilling'
'Wonderful'
'Fulfilling'

## Sensitive Permaculture by Alanna Moore
### - cultivating the way of the sacred Earth
ISBN – 978-0-9757782-2-7

This 2009 book explores the living energies of the land and how to sensitively connect with them. Positive and joyful, it draws on the indigenous wisdom of Australasia, Ireland and elsewhere, combining the insights of geomancy and geobiology with eco-smart permaculture design to offer an exciting new paradigm for sustainable living. It includes the authors experiences of negotiating with the local fairy beings over land use in Australia and Ireland.

Readers say:

*"A delight to read"* Callie

*"You make permaculture so easy and alive---and sweet"* Joy, Taiwan

*"...Hard to put down"* Celia, Permaculture Association of Tasmania

Reviewers comments:

*"A very practical and thoughtful guide for the eco-spiritual gardener, bringing awareness to the invisible dimensions of our landscape"*
Rainbow News, New Zealand

*"An adventure in magical and practical Earth awareness"*
Nexus magazine


## Divining Earth Spirit    by Alanna Moore
### - an Exploration of Global & Australasian Geomancy
2nd edition 2004

ISBN – 978-0-646217000

A global look at geomancy and geobiology from an Australasian perspective, from English ley lines and fairy folk, to geopathic stress and the paradigms of the Aboriginal Dreamtime. The environment is alive and conscious!

*"This book is a classic for anyone wanting to get involved with Earth healing. It contains information by the bucketload... The research that has gone into this book is incredible and no doubt will stir you into wanting to use it yourself"* Radionics Network Vol. 2 No.6

*"Excellent reference book"* Don McLeod, Silver Wheel

*"Love of the topic clearly shows, as Moore brings clarity and a sense of the necessity of personal involvement and engagement with the Earth. The great advantage of Moore's book is in its detailing all the salient aspects of Earth Spirit phenomena....all covered succinctly and with precision... the perfect introduction to the topic."* Esoterica magazine, No. 4, 1995

# The Wisdom of Water by Alanna Moore
ISBN – 978-0-9757782-1-0

Fresh water tends to vanish when human impacts are high. But we can reverse the trend and re-connect with the wisdom and healing powers of water. In this book author Alanna Moore delves into water's mysterious origins and manifestations; its energetic and spiritual aspects; global traditions; as well as water in Australian landscapes. The book is unique in giving holistic understandings about water from a geomancer's perspective, including water divining, historical, esoteric and Indigenous perspectives.

*"Very invigorating... highly recommended"*
Jilli Roberts, PAGAN TIMES Dec 2007

*"A great book!"*
Professor Stuart Hill, Sydney

## Stone Age Farming        by Alanna Moore
- tapping nature's subtle energies for your farm or garden
**(2nd edition, 2012)**

ISBN: 9780975778234

From Irish Round Towers to modern Power Towers for enhancing plant growth. In this book ancient and modern ideas about the energies of rocks and landscapes are explored for practical use in the garden, including the application of dowsing, Earth wisdom, scientific and geomantic understandings  Now, 12 years after its first publication, this is a revised and updated second edition with new photographs and information.

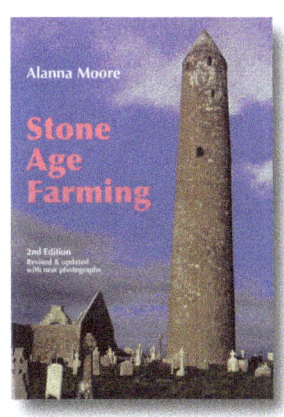

*"Simply fabulous!"*
    Maurice Finkel,  Health and Healing.

*"Quite fantastic."*
    Roberta Britt,  Canadian Quester Journal.

*"Clear, lucid and practical"* Tom Graves

 *"A classic"*    Radionics Network.

*"Will change your perception of the world"*
    Conscious Living magazine

*"A book that gives all of us, whether we tend a small garden, a wild space or a large farm, a way to connect and enhance our space."*
    Barbara Botham, Canadian Society of Dowsers

A Geomantic Guidebook to
# Touchstones for Today  by Alanna Moore
- designing for Earth harmony with stone arrangements and subtle energy dowsing

144 pages, with 90 black & white illustrations
ISBN: 978-0-9757782-5-8

Ancient and enigmatic, the standing stones, labyrinths and stone circles that still haunt various corners of the world have often been subject to systematic destruction. But yet, in some form, they have survived over several millennia. Their enduring presences beg so many questions. How did the ancients manage to erect the huge megalithic monuments, when it is a struggle to replicate them today? For what purposes were they made? They must have been highly significant, given the enormous amount of effort involved. Science and folklore can provide clues. But personal experience of sites and energies detected at sacred stones can be much more revealing and rewarding than bland facts.

Today, sensitive people find that the ancient standing stones, both natural and intentionally placed, can act as transmitters of beneficial Earth energies, providing anchor points for the power and spirit of the land. Not surprisingly, old traditions of healing, divination, wish fulfillment and fertility associated with certain sacred stones continue to find currency today. And anyone may potentially tune in to the sacred stones by taking up the ancient art of dowsing (also known as divining), or other forms of psychic attunement. It can be personally most enriching!

This Guidebook encourages people to discover for themselves the magical and transforming energies associated with both ancient megalithic sites and modern stones of power; and to be inspired to create one's own energetic stone arrangements, as Touchstones of interaction with the Sacred Earth.

*"Moore encourages us to rediscover the ancient wisdom and apply it to our local environments…. Her deep reverence for our sacred Earth is inspiring".*
Ruth Parnell, Nexus magazine, June – July 2013, edition 20-4

*"… a little goldmine of useful information… an easily accessible, concentrated repository of information on all things petrous".*
Grahame Gardner, President of the British Society of Dowsers.

*"The most useful feature of the book is the "do-it-yourself" aspect".*
Kieran Comerford, Irish Society of Diviners

## About the Author
Alanna Moore was a co-founder of the New South Wales Dowsing Society 1984.
A professional dowser, she is internationally known for her writing and teaching of dowsing and geomancy. She lectures worldwide and also makes films. A permaculture farmer and teacher as well, her writings are archived at www.geomantica.com as well as at Australia's National Library.

www.ingramcontent.com/pod-product-compliance
Lightning Source LLC
Chambersburg PA
CBHW082335300426
44109CB00046B/2501